Fi

Lowell, The Acre, and Bobby "The Brawler" Christakos

By

Timothy Imholt, Tom Duggan Jr

With each new wave of immigrants the Acre transforms itself and retains a piece of their heritage. First the Irish then the Greeks and many other ethic groups. Each start businesses that begin to prosper and they move on to other parts of the city making way for the next wave. The Acre is known for tight knit families that live and work in their neighborhood.

Photo: Scott Proposki, PhotosInAMinute.com

The Acre neighborhood exemplifies the plight of immigrants who had little to nothing as they moved to a new country to live the American Dream. The Acre is a place in Lowell that is rich in pride, culture, and diversity.

To anyone from Lowell, that neighborhood represents the struggle of the American spirit. Lowell and its National Historical Park are rich in history as the first industrialized mill city in the United States. The Acre is the first stitch new immigrants sew as they become woven into the fabric of Lowell.

    Lowell Mayor Rodney Elliott – January 25, 201

Fighting Spirit
Copyright © 2015 by Timothy Imholt and Tom Duggan
Valley Patriot Press
PO BO X 453
North Andover, Massachusetts

Front & Back photos: Tom Duggan, Larry Richardson © 2015
Front Photo of Bobby Christakos , Lowell Sun, used with
permission.
Valley Patriot photos and written material used with permission.

For information on this and any book by the authors contact
Tim@TimothyImholt.com
valleypatriot@aol.com

ISBN-13: 978-1507741924
ISBN-10: 1507741928

No part of this book may be reproduced, scanned, or distributed
in any printed or electronic form without written permission.

Fiction Books by Timothy Imholt & David Forsmark

The Forest of Assassins
China Bones Book 1 – China Side
China Bones Book 2 – The Bamboo Caress
China Bones Book 3 – The Red Pagoda
China Bones – The Complete Series

Fiction Books by Timothy Imholt and Michael Garst

The Last World War Volume 1: Trial by Fission
The Last World War Volume 2: Trial by Fusion (in preparation)

Nonfiction Books by Timothy Imholt

Toddler Art

Children's Books by Timothy Imholt

A Collection of Mother Goose Tongue Twisters and Nursery Rhymes

Nonfiction Books by Timothy Imholt & Michael Garst

The Layman's United States Constitution
The Layman's Articles of Confederation
Laughing at a Military Enlistment

Classics with Timothy Imholt Editor/Contributions

A Study in Scarlet with Annotations
The Sign of the Four with Annotations
The Hound of the Baskervilles (Annotated)
The Valley of Fear (Annotated)

Nonfiction Books by Timothy Imholt and Tom Duggan

The Fighting Spirit: Lowell, Bobby Christakos, and The Acre

Introduction

Who is this Boxer named Bobby Christakos?

Why was he known as "The Brawler?"

Why do we care about his story?

To answer that question fully is going to take some effort. We shall try to sum it up quickly, Bobby Christakos is a five time Golden Glove Winner, a proud Greek-American, son of a bookie and is the epitome of a "rising above" story from Lowell Massachusetts and, more specifically, a neighborhood known as The Acre.

To quote Bobby, "Boxing kept me out of prison, my wife, Debra kept me alive."

He is a colorful guy who has done some amazing things in the boxing ring as well as out.

How colorful?

He did win those five titles, but he was also arrested twenty-nine different times...yes, that is accurate, twenty-nine.

He is now a turn-around victory in life, and his life makes a rough parallel with the city of Lowell Massachusetts, his home town. It has had its ups and downs. It has been written off by some people in the past only to turn itself around and show that it, and Bobby, indeed have a bright future.

Special thanks to Bobby for telling us his story and making this book possible.

A very special thank you to Larry Richardson the

owner of the photography studio Drive By Shootings who took many of the pictures we have put in this book. He was patient, easy to work with and helped us mere writers understand what makes a great photograph.

Chapter One

Boxing, Lowell, the Acre, and Bob Christakos

Had it not been for Bobby Christakos' involvement in amateur boxing at an early age, even he will readily admit that he would have ended up in prison. He will also admit that had it not been for his wife he would have wound up dead, with or without, a boxing career.

While the five time New England born and raised Golden Glove Boxing Champion credits his involvement in the sport with saving him from a life of crime, if not direct involvement in organized crime. As it was, he fractured a law or two over the years. However, the boxing industry in the 1970s and 1980s wasn't, necessarily, that much safer than the streets.

Lowell native Bobby Christakos is certainly one of the most colorful people around town. He is one of those guys known to just about everyone. Bobby can walk into a grocery store and five or six people will stop and say hi before he even gets past the front doors. Some of them fans, some critics and some are even police officers who arrested him many years ago, but now that he has turned around, they all love him.

Yes, as much as locals, and even the cops, love Bobby Christakos he's had his bout with the law over the years, something that Bobby says helped shape his outlook on life and on boxing.

How serious were his arrests?

How close was he to going right off that cliff?

Admittedly, some of his interactions with police were over issues that were not that serious. Others, however show how Bobby was heading for a future of jail cells and the discomfort that comes along with such a life.

Retired Police Officer Paul Corcoran and Bobby Christakos clown around while reminiscing about the old days in the Acre.

****

Just to review all his arrests, four were for assault & battery in local bars (a boxer in a bar fight, *what* are the odds), five arrests for disorderly conduct, one arrest for possession of cocaine, one arrest for distribution of illegal narcotics, one arrest for pushing a police officer, and finally one arrest for possession (ok it was consumption) of cocaine in a bar bathroom in full view of an undercover officer.

These brushes with the law were things Bobby readily admits he did, with the exception of one that went to trial where he was found non-guilty, but more on that in a minute, and says it was the stupidity of the time and his inability at times to make better choices for his life. "I screwed up," Bobby says. "I didn't think about tomorrow, I was living in the moment, doing stupid things and not caring about the future or where I would end up."

His arrest record also shows an arrest for stealing the nightly deposit from a store where he was working as a security guard.

"I didn't do it, they knew I didn't do it and I knew I didn't do it. I'm a brawler, I got in fights, I did petty crimes as a kid but I never took that money," Bobby still says, and is obviously still angry about the false accusation.

In the end Christakos was found not guilty by a jury, but he says it still bothers him today.

"I don't care if people want to talk about the dumb things I did, I did them and that's fair. I know it sounds silly now, so many years later but, it that one still bothers me."

Bobby Christakos is right when he says he made a mess of his life for many years. But he also says that he wants to be role model for people who have made mistakes and want to turn their lives around.

Today, among other things, he umpires kid's baseball games, helps kids in the local boxing gyms, and acts as a mentor for troubled youth in Lowell. Bobby Christakos is truly, like his hometown of Lowell Massachusetts, a real survivor. They may keep getting knocked down, but they keep getting right back up, clean themselves off, and have found a better future.

Umpire Bobby Christakos poses with another champ, little league baseball player from Lowell, Zack Beckstein for Callery Park, Lowell (2013).

****

For Bobby or anyone really, growing up in a section of Lowell, Massachusetts called "The Acre" was no picnic back in the 1960s through the 1980s. Even today, it isn't all puppies and rainbows. The Acre was the poorest, most crime ridden neighborhood in the city. A city that was, and in some ways still has, issues with crime and political corruption.

The Acre neighborhood of Lowell was well known for the various forms of criminal activity that plagued the neighborhood. From drug dealing, petty theft, vandalism, and prostitution, to name a few, the crime in the Acre had a crime rate two to three times that of any other part of town.

BOXING IN LOWELL

While Lowell is best known for the thriving textile mills of the late 1800s and early 1900s, the untold success story of Lowell, Massachusetts is The Acre section and how it spawned so many boxers. Of equal importance, it gave birth to some unique and amazing boxing gyms, coaches, tournaments and fans that can't be found in any other neighborhood in the country.

Before becoming the boxing nexus of all New England, Lowell Massachusetts was founded as a planned manufacturing center for textiles back in the 1820s. As a result, for generations, it has fostered a strong, blue-collar community that continues to exist, even today, with skillsets the likes of which could lead an economic recovery for the region, if not the entire nation.

Unlike most cities and towns in America back then, Lowell did not develop organically, one shop, one home at a time. It was a planned city by a group of industrialists who saw a small region twenty-five, or so, miles North of Boston, uniquely situated and chosen for the power provided by the rapids of the Merrimack River to become an industrial center for the region.

For Lowell, the fact that it was once a farming community, only served to make the location all that much more desirable for these early industrialists. It gave their companies, and their workers, a place to buy everything from base products that would eventually become finished goods, to food.

Given that the city was originally formed in the 1820s, before electricity was widely used, the hydroelectric power of the rushing Merrimack River was used to power the massive machines needed to run the vast network of textile mills which served as the main source of non-agricultural employment in the area.

Since those earliest days, Lowell has been known as the scrappy little survivor that never gives up the fight to get better. It has never been a town that just throws in the towel and assumes or accepts the fact that it will always be a crime ridden slum with no hope of revitalization.

Yes, Lowell has been knocked back a number of times but it has never given up. That spirit of Lowell as the underdog who continues the fight turns out to be a very important theme throughout the lives many famous people who were born, and brought up, in the Mill City.

What did the bottom look like for Lowell?

We can debate the history and what specific decades were the worst for the city for many chapters, but the point is that it has had highs and lows. It has gone through a cycle of ups and downs unlike any other city we can find.

Was it when Lowell (and more specifically another

boxer) was featured in an HBO special called High on Crack Street?

Some argue that this particular TV special cast Lowell in such a bad light that it impacted the city's ability to attract new businesses to the area and bring new jobs into the city in the process. But, Lowell didn't throw in the towel.

City leaders cleaned up many of their streets, went to work on reducing crime, and worked to make the city better. While not perfect, and certainly not devoid any of problems, the city of Lowell came together, picked themselves back up, and have built a community that has once again become proud. Gone are many of the major problems that once plagued the city.

Lowell is now a bustling University city filled with college kids, new businesses, one of the best police forces in the country and a has bright future ahead. Make no mistake, Lowell still has its weak points but it has the potential to go all the way and the boxer's attitude to never give up.

In many ways Lowell is very much a boxer, which makes it either ironic or destiny that Lowell's history will include the stories of so many professional and semi-pro fighters to have come out of its' neighborhoods.

How close is that parallel? How often has Lowell almost been down for the count?

Let's answer that question from the beginning.

Lowell, Massachusetts was founded in 1820, yet by the 1850s it was one of the largest industrial complexes in the entire United States. During this period of Lowell's history, she had a good round. People from all over the world immigrated there for a good paying job and better life for their families.

Then the 1930's hit. With the new decade came the great depression that decimated industries far and wide all over the country. Lowell was no exception and, in fact, was hit far worse, and sooner, than most cities and towns across the country. This served to send Lowell into a really bad round.

The Mill City saw a comeback during World War II as the need for textiles grew and were once again being shipped across the globe for the war effort. This was primarily driven by the enormous need that Allied Armies had for parachutes to supply the newly developed Airborne Corps.

After the war the city's growth faded, and Lowell once again fell on hard times. Businesses were slowing down and losing momentum, if not shutting down completely, crime began to rise again, and the city of Lowell began a very steep decline. Another bad round!

Then, as luck would have it, in the 1970s the Mill City became part of a larger statewide recovery as Wang Laboratories started locating many of their research labs in the Lowell area. Chalk up another good round.

Today, as we said, it is a bustling University town filled with college kids, new business and a police force that is second to none. It has a nice balance of arts, industries, and academia, making the city far more stable than it has been in a very long time.

The city is safer today than ever before. City leaders

are cleaning up the streets and even dealing with some of the political or governmental corruption issues, putting it on a winning streak. Lowell officials even took one of their city managers, Brian Martin, to the State Ethics Commission, and had him fired.

In the old days of Bobby Christakos' childhood this kind of political corruption would have been smirked at and gone on without response from local officials. But the city of Lowell fought back against corruption and won a big fight to keep their local government above reproach.

Just like a boxer in the ring who has good rounds and bad, Lowell has had good times and bad. It has good neighborhoods and bad, and it has suffered terrible tragedies and amazing accomplishments. Like a boxer, Lowell pulled itself up, and, surely if history is any guide, will get knocked back down again, but the people of Lowell never give up. They don't know how to solve every problem.

They only know how to keep fighting and keep moving forward. It is truly a town that epitomizes the spirit that has made this nation great.

Like Bobby Christakos, or any other boxer, Lowell repeats that process. The city works hard to get better, then gets back in the fight and tries again when things go bad.

It is this American uniqueness that is exemplified in the people of Lowell, and more particularly in The Acre section of Lowell.

This history is part of why the boxing fans in Lowell are unlike those of almost any other city or town you can visit across the USA. Boxing is a sport where a blue collar guy can get involved, work his ass off, listen to the coaches, and gain some notoriety from coast to coast. Possibly because of this connection, these fans are uniformly well informed, rabid, fun, and supportive of any fighter stepping into the ring from the neighborhood.

They show up for more than just the ability to place a bet or enjoy a fight. They cheer for more than just blood. They cheer good sportsmanship and their local heroes.

Sometimes there is a real rumble worth cheering just for the sake of the rumbling. That was the case the day they got to witness Bobby and his own brother Butch, (who also fought in the Golden Gloves), got into the ring together and not just try to knock each other out, "we tried to kill each other," Bobby says ... they cheered that also.

Multiple boxers from Lowell have told us it was like they weren't brothers but mortal enemies. They went after each other like it was a World War II battlefield and they were both out of ammo.

Bobby won that fight too, at least he claims that is the case.

WHITEY BULGER

The Acre is a neighborhood that has a story much like that of Bobby Christakos, or Micky Ward, or Dickie Ecklund, or any of the other boxers who survived those streets and made it to better times

How the Acre got its name is simple. Many cities in the United States have neighborhoods with specific nicknames. The Acre is a neighborhood that has primarily been the home of Greek and Irish immigrants. To this day if you drive down the streets of that neighborhood it is easy to find Greek restaurants and Irish bars. Some of this heritage has stuck around through until today.

It started out as a single acre of land set aside by the city benefactors. Originally it was just a large number of huts occupied by very poor Irish immigrants. The area grew to be very densely populated and eventually expanded to be much larger than a single acre. Today, Lowell's acre is a great place to get Greek food or find a non-corporate owned bar to grab a few beers and complain about the amount of cold and snow that New England gets in the winter.

When Bobby was growing up it was also the part of town that many parents wouldn't let their kids go to, even during daylight hours. To say it was rough back in those days was putting it mildly.

The Acre was the home of bars, coffee shops, bookie joints (one of which belonged to Bobby's father), nightclubs, convenience stores, row houses, cheap apartments, and, of course, many police calls. The Acre was also a neighborhood where, on any given day, walking the streets you were very likely to bump into a variety of well-known mobsters doing business in the city. One such mobster familiar to the residents of the Acre neighborhood was famed mob boss Whitey Bulger.

Bobby Christakos recounted on 980WCAP radio in 2013 that at a very young age he and Whitey happened to cross paths inside the only bookie joint Bobby was allowed to visit, his fathers. He chuckled as he revealed that it was only so that his father could watch him do his homework. Bobby recalled how he walked into his father's bookie joint one day to see some sort of argument between his dad and Whitey during which the mobster sent young Bobby down the street with a $100 bill to get him a cup of coffee.

Why he wanted a coffee brought into a coffee shop from somewhere else is a mystery, but Whitey was known to be that kind of guy. He wanted to get his hooks into people, to get under their skin, and either annoy them or have them owe him a favor. Possibly both.

"I had no idea who he was, he was just some guy arguing with my father," Christakos says. He says that when he tried to pay for the coffee the girl behind the counter said she didn't have change for a hundred dollar bill, but when he told her it was for some guy named 'Whitey' she told him the coffee was free. Bobby says when he brought back the coffee Whitey told him to keep the money as long as he left so that he could talk to his father.

That was when he says his father stepped in and told the mobster, who is now sitting safely behind bars, to leave his kid alone, throwing Whitey Bulger out of his coffee shop/bookie joint.

Bobby still maintains that he doesn't know what the now famous mobster wanted with his father that day. However, he adds, there are many known cases of this particular mobster walking into a profitable business and attempting to "purchase" it for well below market value, meaning for the price of $0.00. The deal was simple, sell or die.

Looking back, Bobby says once he found out who Whitey was, he was never more proud of his father than on that day.

"To be a successful boxer you have to be really tough," he says. "Having a dad who was willing to stand up to a mobster and throw him out was great training for being a successful boxer who has to survive in the ring."

Bobby's father, Kito, was more than tough; he was fiercely driven to make sure he could care for his family. After his wife passed away at a very young age he had to raise seven kids, on his own. With the income of a coffee shop and bookmaking racket, and living in an environment of illegal betting and racketeering, Bobby's father would stop short of getting directly involved in organized crime.

"He may have bent the occasional law, once in a while," Bobby says laughing, "but he had ethics. It wasn't morality it was just a strong sense of ethics. There were just certain things you didn't do, and that was that."

How far did these ethics go?

One of the more widely known stories about Kito Christakos is about the time he lost a customer for life. Kito knew the man as a regular who loved the gambling offered in the backrooms of the Acre's bars and coffee shops so much that he would show up on payday and not leave until whatever money he had in his pockets was gone.

The fantasy of a huge win causing riches to instantly fall into his lap was just too tempting for this regular customer of the Christakos establishment. One could hardly blame him, given the poverty and rough conditions of the time. Living in that area, working long, hard weeks, and seeing little hope of that changing was frustrating for most living in the Lowell Acre back then. But, while some people take a long term approach to increasing their income from illegal betting, this man clearly needed a quick fix.

One particular day, the man in question, did not make it home to pay his bills before hitting the Acre's "coffee shops" to gamble. As the story goes, his take home pay was about $200 per week and he lost all of his $200 in the Christakos gambling establishment.

Not surprisingly, the man's wife showed up not long after trying to find her husband, and his paycheck. Apparently he had decided to not go home after his hefty loss.

Kito Christakos told the woman that he had long since left and had lost about $200. The woman, shrieking, began to cry explaining that her kids wouldn't be able to eat for a week. When she hysterically asked the elder Christakos what she was supposed to do now, Bobby's dad, being the guy that he was, handed the woman back the $200 and said she could keep it as long as her husband never came back. According to Bobby, once someone was banned from his father's place, that was it, there were no second chances; attempts to return after being banned would not go well for the gambler.

"He wasn't trying to take food away from people, he was just trying to make a living," Bobby recounted to Valley Patriot newspaper publisher Tom Duggan.

Photographer Larry Richardson looks on in background as Bobby Christakos and Paul Murano discuss his boxing career on "Paying Attention! with Tom Duggan" on 980WCAP in Lowell. 2014.

****

Looking back now it's easy to see that the ethics Bobby Christakos got from came from his father, despite the environment they were forced to live in. These translated to sense of fair play and sportsmanship in the younger Christakos that laid the foundation for a successful boxing career.

SPORTSMANSHIP

The art of sportsmanship itself in the boxing ring is critically important. If you are known as a boxer who just wants to climb into the ring and hurt people, rather than competing to win, things are not going to go well for you. Sooner or later someone will come along and hurt you worse than you could ever hurt them and you are finished. That may just translate into a lifelong injury that impacts your life outside the ring.

That wasn't Bobby. That isn't Lowell. Historically speaking, that certainly isn't the United States.

This man, and that town, just want to survive, do the right thing, win from time to time, and of course, have a little fun along the way. He may have walked the line for a while, but he eventually stepped away and made a better life for himself. He credits boxing and, in no small way, his wife for the pivot in his life.

Bobby Christakos was also a troubled kid or, what in today's world some would call an "at risk youth."

He could have gone down many paths; most of them bad, but like Lowell, his ethics, his sense of sportsmanship, and fair play helped him avoid a life in jail and very likely an untimely death.

The same thing goes for Lowell. At several points in its history the city could have buckled its knees and resigned to being an eternally bad, crime-ridden city. It, and Bobby, have managed to avoid this fate over the years.

Why is this important?

It helps to understand how Bobby Christakos got onto the path of becoming a New England Boxing Hall of Fame inductee and it directly chronicles how he got into boxing in the first place.

THE BRAWLER

As a teenager he got into a fist fight outside his father's coffee shop. As Bobby recalls, and we will further detail later, he got his ass kicked ... "badly." Somehow, Bobby's dad found out about the fight and that Bobby had lost. Shortly after Kito Christakos took matters into his own hands.

Bobby Christakos (age 5) with his father, Kito and his dog Rocky outside his father's coffee shop and bookie joint in the Acre neighborhood of Lowell, Massachusetts.

****

Now, in today's world, the typical response would be simple; call the cops, deny any culpability, and sue the pants off the parents of the kid that beat up your son. This was a different world, a different town, and a much different father.

The answer for Bobby's father was simpler, teach Bobby how to fight. "He said, I'm going to train you and you are never going to get your ass kicked again." Bobby's father got him to the boxing gym every day and made him get in shape, trained him to fight and worked him hard so that he didn't have to worry about his son's safety in the rough and tumble Acre neighborhood they lived and worked in.

Bobby's eyes light up as he recounted what happed a year later when he came across that very same kid who gave him the beating of his life.

As he tells it, the second round went a much differently than the first, despite the fact that Bobby was a few years younger and much smaller than his opponent.

From those early days Bobby was a brawler.

Shortly after getting into the sport recreationally, Bobby entered organized boxing. He went from the Silver Gloves, later into the Golden Gloves, a few fights as a professional, and if a traffic accident had not ended his fighting career he may very well have won a world title.

If you aren't familiar with the Silver or Golden Gloves, never fear we will explain them, and many other boxing terms, in a bit.

The story of boxing, the story of Lowell, and the story of Bobby are very much like the story of America. You can hit us, you can even knock us down, you might even win a fight, maybe two, but we get back up, we train harder, prepare more, and we come back in that next fight much more prepared. For our nation, this extends from the sports to the industrial, intellectual, political, or any other walk of life. We are competitive by nature and like to be the best at what we do.

This book will follow Bobby, Lowell, boxing in Lowell, and try (for those not familiar with the sport) to understand the appeal for boxing. Below is our Bobby Christakos in 2014 goofing off in the ring at Art Ramalho's West End Gym with Dickie Ecklund, who is also a former Professional and Golden Glove boxer, as well as the brother of former World Champion Micky Ward, who, after all these years, still doesn't follow all of the rules.

Mickey Ward and Bobby Christakos mix it up in the ring, 2014.

Chapter Two

What is boxing and what are the rules?

What the heck is boxing anyway?

We hear about it.

We see it on television (ok pay per view) from time to time.

We even watch movies that focus on people who have taken part in it.

Other than two people beating the crap out of each other, with a referee who appears to try and enforce some set of mysterious rules, what the heck is boxing?

What are the rules?

What is the scoring system?

This chapter will attempt to answer all of these questions and more. If you are already familiar with the sport, feel free to move to the next chapter. We are gearing this chapter for the casual fan who wants to know more, or even for someone who may know next to nothing about the sport.

Boxing, at a fundamental level, is a sport of personal combat. It involves two people in a ring, engaged in a physical contest which tests strength, speed, reflexes, endurance, strength of will, and tolerance for stress. Put simply, it does all of this within the framework of a certain set of rules while the two competitors throw punches at each other wearing gloves custom made for this purpose.

The hope of every fighter you will ever meet is to get a knockout. A "knockout" in the sport one of the two fighters doesn't really need to be knocked unconscious, although that has happened. They only need to be knocked down, and unable to stand without assistance, for a count of ten seconds.

The sport of boxing is broken down into amateur and professional boxing. In both levels of the sport, boxers can't simply go at each other until someone is knocked out. There may be sports where that happens, some back alley bare knuckle fights masquerading as boxing for instance, but that isn't the organized sport we are discussing. True boxing matches are broken up into rounds.

Depending on the level of boxing there are some number of rounds extending from one to twelve. The rounds vary from one to three minutes in length with a period of rest in between so that each fighter can to catch their breath, get some pointers from their trainers, and far more importantly, regroup a little for the next round.

The fight continues until the referee counts an opponent out thereby declaring him knocked out, a boxer is deemed unable to continue by a referee in some other fashion, is disqualified for breaking a rule, resigns by throwing in the towel, or one of the fighters is declared the winner by the judge's scorecards at the end of the last round.

When did this sport begin?

Surely it is an invention of modern man who just wanted to watch two people bludgeon one another.

As a sport, boxing can be traced back to Ancient

Greece, which Bobby would probably argue is the reason so many Greek-Americans, like himself, have mastered the sport.

The sport goes so far back, and been so well documented, in fact, that we know for certain that the first known appearance of boxing in the Olympic Games was around 650BC, some 2,600 years ago, meaning that the sport is considerably older. Boxing has evolved over the years, and in the process it has gained a great deal of formality and popularity. Much of this formality began in the 18th century as the sport evolved into modern prize fighting around the middle of the 19th century.

For many centuries boxing was a sport found primarily in army camps when people weren't training with swords or other weapons more deadly than fists. Then, at long last, around 1740 or so a formalized set of rules showed up in England. These eventually came to be known as the Broughton's rules.

One of the rules that the fighters of those days enjoyed that someone entering boxing today would just love to have is what we will call the one knee rule. If a fighter were to drop to one knee they would get a 30-second count (like a time out) at any given point during the match. This could be invaluable if someone were out of breath and needed a moment to regroup their thoughts on how to proceed against a particularly tough opponent. Eventually this rule was thrown out as many competitors viewed it as "unmanly" deciding instead that any boxer who couldn't continue and needed half a minute should just throw in the towel and quit. The modern boxers we met would have used a whole different series of words to describe someone that did this; unmanly would have been the nicest one of those.

Not all of the rules of the day versus those used in modern boxing favored the fighters of these centuries. In fact, some of the modern rules have prevented some of the extensive injuries that were commonplace in these early boxers. These fighters did not have gloves with wrist straps to protect their hands.

Think about this for a second. These were bare knuckle boxers. The hand is full of very small bones. The head is one of the primary targets in boxing and the head is full of protective, large, and very hard bones. Bones actually do come in different a variety of hardnesses. The ones in the head are protective plates. Think of them like armor for the brain. If you boxed often and threw hard punches you could cause extensive damage to your hands. This is a problem some retired modern boxers still complain of so one can only imagine how bad the problem would be without these gloves.

Just as a momentary aside, it seems relevant to point out something about our brawling boxer, Bobby Christakos. When doing research for this book many people spoke on the record about sparring (practicing) with Bobby. One of those was former boxing World Champion Micky Ward. Micky, also of Lowell, says that Bobby Christakos had one of the hardest heads he ever hit.

In fact, Micky admits, and Bobby brags, that while sparring with Micky one day, he sprained something in his hand, through the gloves while punching Bobby in the head. Bobby just smiled and kept coming back at him. Now, to be fair Bobby was about 20 pounds heavier than Micky at the time but to take the hit from a future (at that point) champion in the head, smile, and keep coming? Micky said it was just unheard of.

Many people have told us that Micky has a punch that comes from the left like no one else in his weight class. In other words, to take that hit, and smile, well that says something about your ability to take a punch. Taking a punch is something very necessary in the sport.

Basically, the point is that the man has a very hard head. Everyone we have spoken to says he is a stubborn guy but to sprain the wrist of a future world champion with your face? Now THAT is one hard head.

EVOLUTION OF BOXING IN THE MODERN CENTURIES

In the 1830s the English transformed the rules of boxing a bit. In 1838 there was an official publication the London Prize Ring rules formalizing the modern sport. These were later revised in 1857 but made several changes to the sport:

- Fights would occur in a 24 feet square ring surrounded by ropes.

- If a fighter was knocked down he had to get up in 30 seconds. This rise had to be under his own power (he couldn't hold onto the ropes) before the fight was allowed to continue. If he was unable to do so he would be declared knocked out.

- Biting was declared illegal

  - o Do you hear that Mike Tyson? Ok, we couldn't resist. Mike, please don't hit us, we have women and kids who love us, think of the children!!!!

- Head butting was declared illegal

- Hitting below the belt was declared illegal

  - o Hear that Dicky Eklund? Ok, we actually put him up to the hit you saw in the picture at the end of Chapter One but it was fun to call him out anyway, he is really an amazing guy and doesn't deserve the hard time people give him.

These rules remained in effect for about a decade, and remain, more or less, part of the sport today, with some modification.

The next major evolution of the rules was in 1867 when the so-called Marquess of Queensberry rules were written, published, and widely circulated. These rules became the new law of the land with regard to organized fighting.

Within these transformations there were a total of twelve new rules for boxing. They specifically said that fights should be "a fair stand-up boxing match" in a 24-foot-square ring. Rounds were formally set at three minutes with a one minute rest period in between. If a fighter was knocked down they now had only 10-seconds to get back up, and any kind of wrestling was banned.

These new rules also formalized the use of gloves of a "fair size." The use of gloves totally changed the sport.

Gone were the days of someone destroying their hands just for the sake of the sport.

Gone were the days of someone being killed in the ring on a fairly regular basis.

As a result of the use of gloves fights became longer, and more strategic in nature. A great deal more importance was being placed on defense. Movements in the ring such as slipping and bobbing became commonplace and very necessary. As a result of these new rules, and especially thanks to the gloves, what we now know as modern boxing emerged.

Through the latter half of the 1800s boxing was not widely considered to be a legitimate sport. At one point it was even outlawed in all of England and large portions of the United States. The only place that a fight could be seen was at a less than legitimate gambling establishments and if these were discovered, they would often be broken up by the police. This was a time when fight organizers would, from time to time, put local police on the payroll and in turn they would look the other way. Some have argued that this was the start of organized crime infesting the sport of boxing.

Throughout this time, because of the lack of official sanctions, legality, and other forms of legitimate organization, the rules of boxing itself were often disregarded. Fighters would often resort to wrestling tactics. Two fighters "going the distance" was a rare occurrence and fights in the crowd, or even riots breaking out, were very common.

Eventually these fights, which can only be described as backroom brawls, gave way to boxing becoming a sport of some popularity in the twentieth century. In the modern sense boxing is back to having rules, and to this day the general Marquess of Queensberry rules are still used, with some minor changes here and there, but these classic rules still provide the framework for the sport in the 21st century.

THE POINT SYSTEM

Officially, according to today's rules, there is a panel of judges to score each fight. The official rules state that there can be up to three judges, and this is the part of boxing that gets controversial if not absolutely confusing. These judges are there to assign points to boxers for various things happening in the ring, for example, landing a punch.

It is this scoring system that only becomes important if both boxers go the distance or, in other words, they finish the final round without a knockout.

The points making up the total score are assigned based on punches that connect, how well a boxer performs on defense, and, of course, any knockdowns. That all sounds great but it doesn't come without major controversy. There are other, much more subjective ways in which a judge can assign, or even take away points from a fighter during a fight. For example, they have been known to take points off if a fighter repeatedly hits below the belt, which is forbidden. This is where fighters have said to be "robbed" of a victory.

There are, of course, cases where the judges noticed something the crowd didn't and took off points, leading to more controversy.

Historically there are also documented cases where a judge or two was on the payroll of someone (possibly a mobster) and a close call went the way of the guy making the payoff. In today's fights judges are watched closely, at least at the professional level, so these kind of things are reasonably close to non-existent, at least at that level. Now, at the local and amateur level…who can say for sure?

The judges rule the ring. In the case of a fight that does not end in a knockout no amount of arguing with judges will cause a decision to be changed. This is why most fighters cherish the knockout. Winning a fight by knockout leaves no doubt as to the victor.

Amateur boxing departs from professional in a number of ways. In general, the rules are the same with some minor changes, all of which are meant to protect the amateur fighters so that they can learn without suffering career ending injuries early on.

One departure is that typically amateur (e.g. Olympic, Golden Glove) bouts are limited to three or four rounds. Scoring is calculated based on the number of clean blows landed, regardless of quality of impact, where in professional fights quality matters.

One of the major, more recent, changes in amateur boxing is that fighters must wear protective headgear. This serves to reduce the number of injuries, as well as the number of knockdowns and ultimately knockouts. This is a big reason why professional boxing remains far more popular than amateur boxing. Boxing fans find it far more exciting when there are more knockdowns and knockouts in the ring.

When research for this book began a large number were more than happy to talk about Bobby Christakos. He was referred to as "basher" and a "brawler". In fact, many of Bobby's friends have said that his brawling style has been part of his life outside the ring as well.

That leads one to understand that there are different styles of boxing and different kinds of boxers. For those who do not know much about them a few of the former boxers who spoke of Bobby Christakos outlined what the differences are. There are a lot more styles of boxers and boxing than anyone would think.

THE CLASSIC

The first is generally referred to as a classic boxer.

This is a style characterized by keeping as much distance as possible between you and your opponent. Personally, after meeting some of these guys, if you find yourself in the ring with them, distance sounds like a great idea. Watching them hit the heavy bag makes one wonder if typical human ribs could take it.

The classic boxer keeps their distance and depends mainly on faster, longer-range punches. These are usually jabs as this style of classic boxing is used to wear down an opponent.

These types of classical fighters typically win by decision, (points from the judges) not by knockout. Classic fighters would often be the guys who likes to taunt their opponents over a large number of rounds and tire them out. In other words, if you know you have more stamina than your opponent this is a great tactic to use.

These guys tend to be more skilled than some of the other styles but you have to have a reach longer than your opponent not to mention be faster in delivering your punches and have excellent reflexes to get out of trouble quickly. This is NOT the style of boxing Sylvester Stallone used in the Rocky movies. This was more of the fictional character Apollo Creed's style of boxing.

THE PUNCHER

There is also a style of boxer known as a puncher, or a boxer/puncher. These are fighters who can also fight at close range with a series of combinations. This style results in more knockouts as a result of the combination or sometimes, a single really powerful shot.

One of the most well known fighters in the world, Muhammad Ali, is thought to be a prime example of both of these styles of fighting. He was capable of exhibiting several boxing styles, and could switch between them quickly. That was one of the reasons he was a Champion. This ever changing style, as well as his outside the ring antics, allowed him to get inside other fighters heads.

Boxing Champion Micky Ward says (and we are paraphrasing) that if a fighter gets in your head it can be worse than a series of well-delivered body shots. Muhammad Ali could get in people's heads weeks before the fight even started.

According to Micky, when that happens your adrenaline level skyrockets hours before the fight starts, you get nervous and you burn a ludicrous amount energy. All of this is before the first bell rings starting round one. What Micky taught us is that boxing is as much a mental sport as it is physical. If you lose the mental aspect you may as well just go home. In Micky's words Ali was "capable of f&!#ing with your head for days before the fight." Looking back at Ali's press conferences he was a master, one can see how true that had to be for an opponent.

COUNTER PUNCHERS

Counter Punchers are a defensive type of fighter. These are the boxers who wait for their opponents to make a mistake, and then find a way to take advantage of that mistake. They typically utilize their ability to block shots, to bide time looking for an opening (or their opponent to get tired). If you step in the ring with one of these guys you have to be very good at not telegraphing attacks. Counter Punchers are good at watching and are known to be very patient. If that is combined with an awesome left hook, it could knock you on your butt before you know what it was that hit you.

This style offers those who use it a pretty big advantage. In the act of counter punching a boxer gets to use the forward momentum of the opponent, who just missed their shot, against them. In other words their own missed punch, their own spent energy drives them into your fist. As a result of this, knockouts are far more common using this style than some may think.

THE BRAWLERS

This brings us to Brawlers. Bobby Christakos is a Brawler. So, for that matter is another famous boxer by the name of George Foreman. Long before George sold all of us a grill that makes great burgers, he was a fantastic brawler.

Foreman, in fact, was a World Champion brawler who also fought Muhammad Ali for the World Heavyweight Championship in one of the most famous fights of all time. It is known as The Rumble in the Jungle.

The fight took place in Zaire on the continent of Africa. Ali won the fight but it took him eight rounds and if you have never seen a video of the fight it was a real show. At one point, looking at these guys in the corners between rounds seven and eight, it looked like both trainers wanted to throw in the towel. Anyone interested in the sport of boxing should find a recording of that fight and watch for themselves.

YouTube is a great resource for this sort of thing.

A Brawler is possibly the most feared style of fighter in the sport of boxing. These are guys like George Foreman, Rocky Marciano, Sonny Liston, Micky Ward (early on in his career, later he became far more refined in his style), Bobby Christakos as well as the fictional Rocky Balboa from the Rocky movies.

An autographed photo of Billy Ryan and Rocky Marciano from Bobby's collection of boxing memorabilia.

These are fighters who lack finesse and generally have no real ability to do any kind of fancy footwork. They make up for it with the ability to take a punch, and in return, punch amazingly hard. Lots of the Brawlers that have been in the sport over the years tend to ignore any kind of combination punches and instead tend to pound their opponents with slower moving, but far more powerful single punches.

The most vital assets a Brawler must have are power and a strong chin. These are the guys that tend to let other people just punch them over and over again and take it. Bobby was certainly this style of fighter. Looking at our friend's nose then and now it is hard to miss…Sorry Bobby we had to point out that you used to be prettier, at least we hope so. Brawlers tend to take two or three hits to one that they deliver. It is important for a brawler to win by knockout as they are usually behind on points throughout the fight.

THE SWARMER

The last style of fighter we want to mention is the swarmer. These are pressure fighters that stay in close to their opponent. They tend to throw intense fast moving combinations of punches. These boxers also tend to have very hard chins, as being close in on their opponent at all times means they will get hit more often. This is the style of fighting that shorter boxers tend to use as their arms are not as long as their opponents.

Anyone who watches the many films of Micky Ward fights will see that he tended to be a combination Brawler and Swarmer. Bobby on the other hand was much slower than Micky and tended to just be a Brawler. Bobby says he loves the fact that his style was pure bar-fight style brawling. Perhaps that is why he was arrested for bar fights so often over the years. Might there be a connection there? Alcohol…a boxer…that might explain a few things, and when you ask Bobby about this he just puts up his hands in surrender and says, "guilty" with laugh.

TYPES OF PUNCHES

While there are various styles of boxing, and boxers, there are also different types of punches.

Each type of punch depends on a different set of muscles, and some fighters are naturally better at one than the others. All of these types of punches will be thrown into the dialogue by announcers, but for those who are unfamiliar with them let us explain them briefly.

- The *uppercut* is a punch that originates very low and comes up to impact the opponent, usually in the chin. This can work its way through certain types of defenses and can be the end of a fight if a boxer doesn't have a hard chin.

- A *cross* is a powerful punch that goes for the chin, it crosses the fighter's body and travels toward the opponent in a relatively straight line. The rear shoulder is thrust forward and finishes the movement just touching the outside of the chin. This punch gains additional power as the torso and hips are rotated as the cross is thrown. This type of punch, used properly, has been responsible for more than one broken jaw.

- A *hook* is a punch that travels in a semi-circle and is typically, although not always, at the head. The non-punching hand is typically tucked against the jaw in an effort to protect the chin as this type of punch does leave you open otherwise. It gains additional power from the hips which are rotated.

- The *jab*. This is widely recognized as the most important punch in a boxer's bag of tricks. It gives him a fair amount of protection and leaves the least ability for an opponent to counter punch. It is a quick punch thrown with the lead hand from a guarded position. The fist typically rotates 90 degrees and will be more or less horizontal upon impact.

Defense is what, to most rational people, would be the most important part of boxing. After meeting a large number of people who have stepped into the ring, including a number of former world champions of various weight classes we would really want to know how to protect ourselves from these guys. Either that or you would want them on your side in a bar fight.

There are a number of basic protective tricks a fighter can use, and we would like to sum them up in the following way:

- The clinch – Clinching is when a boxer wraps his arms around the outside of the opponent's shoulders so no one can throw a punch. The referee will come break them apart and put some distance between them. This is used by a fighter in trouble to gain some distance and regroup.

- The Cover-up – Covering up with your hands is pure defense. It is almost impossible to throw a punch from this position, but you can protect your head from a flurry of incoming hits.

- The Block – This is when a boxer uses his shoulder or hands to stop an incoming attack. Whatever body part is put in the way of the hit stops it from coming in, usually when it isn't full force, and protects the head and body from the blow. This can be particularly useful if you have been pounded in the head for five rounds. Blocking one can really turn your mental game around. Now if only our friend

Bobby could have done that. He tended to block them with his face but several people who sparred him said he had the hardest head there was, so it was ok. He says that it was a great way to get inside someone's head. If you get hit in the face and smile at the guy who hit you it was completely demoralizing.

- <u>Bob and weave</u> – This is when the head is moved laterally or below an incoming punch. As the punch comes in the fighter quickly moves his head out of the way.

- <u>Sway</u> – If you can anticipate where a punch is coming from you can move your upper body or head out of the way so that the punch either misses or hits in a way so that the force is much less.

- <u>Slipping</u> – This is something every boxer we talked to said that Bobby was absolutely no good at. When asked about this, Bobby said it was part of his game. "Let them hit me, smile, and keep coming would freak them out." For anyone else, volunteering to take the hit is crazy talk, but not to Bobby. The slip is when the body is rotated slightly to avoid an incoming hit. This is typically a maneuver of the head as a punch comes in the fighter will rotate quickly making the punch "slip" past. In the early days, Mike Tyson was very good at this.

Two important items remain.

THE TRAINERS

Who the heck are all those guys in the corner in between rounds?

It looks hilarious if you think about it. A guy is in the ring for a few minutes beating up or getting beaten, then a bunch of guys with a stool come into one of the corners of the ring. They proceed to rub him, dump water on him, mess with his face, shout instructions, and in some ways seem to annoy him. What is the point? What purpose do they serve?

There are normally four people in the corner between rounds. The first is the boxer whose role is obvious. The second is the trainer and the assistant trainer. The final person is the cutman. The cutman doesn't cut the boxer. His job is to make sure that any cuts on the boxer's face and eyes are closed as much as possible.

It is these three men that will typically call the fight, or throw in the towel, if they deem a boxer should not continue. The boxer gets a say, but typically a trainer will stop the fight if the boxer is in danger, regardless of what the boxer says about it.

Finally, the difference between Silver Gloves (or mittens), Golden Gloves, Olympic, and Professional Boxing. Also what are all these weight classes we hear about and how are they broken down?

The Silver Mittens, or Silver Gloves, as it is officially called, is an annual amateur boxing competition here in the United States. It is for people between the ages of 10 and 15.

The Golden Gloves picks up where the Silver Gloves stops and is for boxers age 16 and over.

The Olympics are an obvious international competition that every fighter early on in their career wants to be in. Everyone wants to bring home that Olympic Gold. It would be the thrill of a career to be able to do so.

Professional boxing matches are the fights we all watch on television where the champions in the various weight classes are determined.

WEIGHT CLASSES

The final thing in this chapter is very simple. We hear terms like featherweight, heavyweight, and so forth but what do they mean?

We will offer up the following breakdown for the Olympic Style and Amateur Boxing are as follows:

1. Light Flyweight – Max 106-lbs

2. Flyweight – Max 112-lbs

3. Bantamweight – Max 119-lbs

4. Featherweight – Max 125-lbs

5. Lightweight – Max 132-lbs

6. Light Welterweight – Max 141-lbs

7. Welterweight – Max-152-lbs

8. Middleweight – Max-165-lbs

9. Light Heavyweight – Max-178-lbs

10. Heavyweight – Max-201-lbs

11. Super Heavyweight – Max is unlimited

For the Professional men's and women's weight

classes:

1. Strawweight
    a. Men's Max-105-lbs
    b. Women's Max-102-lbs
2. Mini Flyweight
    a. Men's Max-Not Applicable
    b. Women's Max-105-lbs
3. Junior Flyweight-(From here forward it is both genders) Max-108-lbs.
4. Flyweight – Max-112-lbs
5. Super Flyweight – Max-115-lbs
6. Bantamweight – Max-118-lbs
7. Super Bantamweight – Max-122-lbs
8. Featherweight – Max-126-lbs
9. Super Featherweight – Max-130-lbs
10. Lightweight – Max-135-lbs
11. Super Lightweight – Max-140-lbs
12. Welterweight – Max-147-lbs
13. Super Welterweight – Max-154-lbs
14. Middleweight – Max-160-lbs
15. Super Middleweight – Max-168-lbs
16. Light Heavyweight – Max-175-lbs
17. Cruiserweight – Max-200-lbs
18. Heavyweight – Unlimited

In the following chapters, among other things, we will discuss some of the fights Bobby had over the years in, and out, of the ring. We will find that boxing, and Bobby's career, have been a great metaphor for the city of Lowell and even more so for the Acre, and that perhaps we can all learn something form a boxer. Never give up, when you get knocked down, train harder, get back up, get back in the ring, and try again. Never consider this to be your last fight, and never, ever, say you can't win. That is how Champions are born.

This photo is Bobby Christakos, our 5-time Golden Glove Winner, in the center with Micky Ward on the right who was a world champion in his weight class, and Bo James, who was also a boxer, when they happened to run into one another at the opening of Jim McNally's gym. Jim is a former boxer himself who has recently retired from the United States Secret Service.

BO JAMES

Interesting sideline story about Bo James. He is older than Bobby by about a decade. When Bobby started learning how to box, Bo James was one of the people he would spar with. Bo was already fighting in the Golden Gloves and considering turning pro. Normally a guy like that would take it easy on a young guy. Not Bo. He never stopped giving Bobby what he gave everyone, he never cut him any slack.

Bo claims that the moment you do that, people think the sport is easy. If you give them your best every time they will train harder, or find some other way to fill their time and vacate the boxing gym for someone willing to commit to the sport. Training harder is the key. If you aren't willing to work hard, this is not the sport for you.

Chapter Three

The boxing brother

In order to better understand Bobby Christakos, or even the city of Lowell, it is necessary to get an idea of the kind of family Bobby came from. Lowell is the kind of city where families stuck together.

In chapter one we learned a little bit about his father. There is a whole story of his father, and that time period in Lowell which probably deserves its own book. There are connections to the mafia inside the city government, organized crime connected to big businesses, political corruption, and the eventual cleanup of the city. We will try to tell some of that story in this book, but only in broad strokes. Someday, especially the mafia story, will be a book.

Today, however, this isn't Lowell. That part of the city's history is just that...history, but it is history worth learning about and learning from.

Bob was one of seven kids.

Who were these other kids?

What were they like?

By all accounts they were like Bobby. They were fighters. They fought, and continue to fight, for what they believe in, and well...sometimes just for fun. This is not uncommon in Lowell during that time. As we said, this is a town where families stuck together. They may fight with one another now and again, but rarely would you find that "disowned" or "estranged" child, brother, sister, whatever. Families stuck together and given the times they really had to. They depend on one another for everything. Lowell isn't an amazingly affluent town, the people who live there may not have had a lot, but they do have one another.

Bobby's younger brother, Butchy, was also a boxer in the Golden Gloves. Butchy, himself, fought his way to three local or regional Golden Glove titles bringing the family total to eight.

Butchy's fighting weight was normally around 165-lbs. He had a real take no prisoners attitude in the ring, as well as in life. From the moment the bell would ring he would come directly at his opponent and, he would not stop putting on pressure until one of them was down.

Many of the people he had been in the ring with were known to say that after you were in a fight with Butch…you knew it. You didn't just wake up the next day ready for anything. It was a fight that involved being sore for a long while, and Butch was an amateur.

Butchy was a tough guy outside the ring too, much like his brother, and the town. In the early 1980s when he, and his older brother were fighting through the Golden Gloves, Lowell was the kind of city that raised a tough breed of people. Some of the guys could be paving streets or working construction during the day, and boxing at night. It was a town of bar fights, street fights, and where people would actually fist fight the guy that stood their sister up for a date. They were tough, but had their standards.

Butchy trained in the West End gym alongside his brother and in those days a large number of other boxers of some notoriety, like Micky Ward, and Dickie Eklund. Many of these guys were working under the watchful eye of the former horse trainer, turned boxing gym owner, Art Ramahlo at the West End gym on Lawrence Street overlooking the very river that was responsible for building the industrial base in the town. By any standard, there was a real concentration of talent in that particular gym. So much so that one can't help but say that it was Art Ramahlo that was a big part of why.

One thing you will never fully understand by speaking with the humble Mr. Ramahlo, but others have told us repeatedly, is that Art is a special kind of guy. Lowell was a town, and in some ways still has, a large number of at risk kids. Art gave them a place to go, taught them to stay out of trouble, rarely can a curse word be heard in his gym, and he always made sure these kids had food to eat. He cared about his fighters and cares as much today as ever, as he continues to train fighters and helps organize the Lowell Sun Golden Glove Tournament every year.

After speaking with Art he would never say this was true. But what is true is that athletes can be talented, they can even have drive, but the other part of that equation is coaching. Without proper coaching, and the ability to listen to that coaching, any athlete will not reach their full potential.

Bobby, according to many accounts, including from people who don't like him very much, could have gone much further if he would have listened better. Micky Ward had several attempts at turning professional and says it was only after he started listening to trainers more that he started to achieve status as more than "the kid on the rise" to become the World Champion. It was more than just listening that was important, but so was drive, desire, in addition to the ability to work with the team that helped him train. Bobby had everything but also had that super hard head that we heard about.

Bobby, and Butch had a ton of talent. They had the right coach. Butch had no desire to turn pro; he just wanted to see what he could do in the ring. Bobby, well, we will discuss that, but all in good time.

Back in January of 1982 Dennis Whitton wrote one of the earliest newspaper articles about Butchy Christakos' boxing career. In that article he said something about Butchy and his fighting spirit that held true for both Christakos brothers, certainly holds true for the people of Lowell, and has a resemblance to the spirit that formed this country.

He called Butchy a hungry tiger in the ring.

In the wild, a tiger has a very specific hunting style. A tiger gets in as close as it can to its target. Once in position it jumps, usually from behind, and mauls its next meal to death in one motion. Butchy would do the same thing in the ring. He would get in close, just out of arm's reach of his opponent, move in quickly, get in close, and throw vicious combinations to the body, to the head, to any open target.

The fight that drew this comparison was against James "Too Tall" Tarantino. Even this early on in his career, much like a tiger, he was down to Earth and serious at all times. He concentrated, he would stare down opponents, and he would never get distracted. Some fighters become known for showboating, not

Butch, that wasn't his style.

Butch was the first fight of the night. His opponent had a huge reach advantage. That was no problem for Butch. He kept the man against the ropes with his aggressive style. Butch went inside and just pounded away. He was throwing combinations to the body, to the head, back to the body, anywhere he could inflict some pain.

Butch won that early fight; it was a split decision from the judges. There was no knockout that night, but that was ok, Butch had one for the win column.

After the fight, in an interview, he was asked how he won…how he prepared. Well, at the time his older brother Bobby was the defending AAU champ for his weight class. Butch said that between his father and his brother pushing him to train there was no excuse to not be in good enough shape to stay in the fight. He had these two helping with his training every single day.

He had some other help the night of that particular fight. He suffered from a real problem with nerves prior to the fight. It was his first time in the tournament; it was the first fight that mattered. There were other fighters from the West End Gym around, all supporting each other. It was Micky Ward, still an amateur fighter at the time, who was in the back of the room that night. Micky wasn't even fighting that night; he was just there supporting his friends. That night he helped out Butch by getting him over his nerves, maintain focus, and be mentally prepared to step into the ring.

Remember, this was Butch's first night in the Golden

Gloves. Anyone would be nervous under those circumstances. Sure he had seen his brother go through this before, but it is different when it is your face that could be smashed in.

He was successful that night, partially thanks to his takes no prisoners, and never quit attitude. He was also a winner that night because he had people on his team that he listened to. In other words the younger Christakos fought, not with the same style as Bobby, but he did have one thing in common. Pure heart.

There was no thought of the word quit.

Just like the city of Lowell, or even the United States, there was no giving up hope. There was never a time when all was lost. Even when out-matched physically that night Butch wouldn't stop until he was victorious.

But, Butch was just getting started.

Remember the fight we just learned about was in early January of 1982. This next fight was a quick one month later in early part of February of that same year.

This next fight was against Joe Poretta for a three round bout, which is typical in the Golden Gloves.

It was a back and forth fight the entire night. Joe was winning, Butch was winning, and then Joe would again take the lead. There would be blows to the head, to the body, sweat poured from both men, and until the end of the second round it was anyone's fight.

At the end of that second round both men went back to their own corner to sit on the stool and go through the between rounds activities. Both appeared ready to throw in the towel and go home to get some rest. At the very least they would both head to a bar to find a way to deaden the throbbing bruises.

Then, suddenly, it was time for round three. Butch and Joe went back to work. It was obvious both men were exhausted, barely able to raise their hands. Butch got in close and went right back to work. It was a pure test of wills and Butch was going to win, he didn't care how tired he was. He might barely be able to lift his hands, but when he did they were going to land somewhere on his opponent. He didn't appear to care much about where.

Butch won that fight by decision. That night was in question until the final seconds when he went to work again with a series of combinations that seemed to come from nowhere.

How could he have had the energy?

This man had no energy, he just forced himself to go on and win. That burst of energy, right at the end, forced him into the lead on points, and the decision was unanimous. Butch was the winner.

It was a long summer in 1982. Butch went on to fight many other amateur fights, gaining experience, some bumps, some bruises and a few hundred dollars a night for his efforts.

If we fast forward to November of that same year it was time for the New England regional AAU Championships. Butch was going to fight that night, his brother was a defending Champ (in a different weight class), and so this was Butch's night to prove his ability to contribute to the family legacy.

On a crisp, clear night in early November Butch was on a ticket that contained other fighters from the West End Gym like future Champion Micky Ward.

Micky lost that night to Dave Attardo by a split decision, but came back years later and became the World Champion and today is a humble man who still trains fighters in various weight classes from Florida to Massachusetts.

Why does Micky come into this story, other than having trained in the same gym, having fought that night, and coming out of Lowell?

It turns out in preparation for that night; Butch was looking for sparring partners. It would seem that with all of the gifted amateurs and professionals coming from that place it would be easy for him to find someone to step into the ring with. That is, assuming pads are used, and if we were getting in the ring with any of these guys there would be a LOT of pads involved.

Butch hit hard, he could box, he could fight like a brawler, he had style, he could switch things up, he could confuse an opponent, and did we mention that he could hit really hard?

He was so good, so serious about the craft, trained so hard, that no one at the West End Gym, including future World Champion Ward, would spar with him anymore. The guys at the gym said it would be like risking life and limb.

That is, almost no one. Butch's big brother Bobby would never leave his brother hanging, looking for experience that can only be gained by sparring with someone. Despite being the defending Amateur

57

Champ Bobby, to this day, says it was some of the most painful sparring he did in his entire life.

To quote Bobby, "It was like he wasn't my brother."

Other boxers from the West End Gym say they remember that summer when these two guys would try to kill each other. None of the trained athletes in that gym wanted to even get in there and try to separate them.

On the night of November 4, 1982, Butch fought Jose Miguel. Jose had more experience and a much longer reach than Butch. That didn't matter. Butch, being the level headed tiger he was, lured Jose into fighting the traditional Christakos close-in brawling style. That was to the demise of Jose.

The first round was taken up by these two trying to figure out how to fight one another. The second round was a much different story. It was head to head, no clear leader, no one breaking out...then Butchy landed a hard right cross and Jose was out for a count of eight. No one saw it coming. He had waited for an opening, when he found it he pounced.

The remainder of the fight was pure Butchy. In the third and final round he landed a vicious combination that staggered Jose, and he almost knocked the man out. The fight did go to the end of the third. There would be no knockout that night, but the score cards made Butch the unanimous victor and thus he captured the 96th Annual New England AAU Golden Gloves 165-pound title.

With that win he was to have just one more fight before he could be off to the Nationals. Yet another kid from Lowell with great potential, no one knew where he would go or what he could do in the ring. But he was always entertaining and the crowd loved him.

The entertainment portion of boxing is something the great ones never forgot. Butch had them, he had the crowd. That is vital for a fighter. If you have the crowd and you can get in your opponents head you can go far. If you allowed your opponents to get inside of your head, that was the end for you.

Without a doubt one of the most popular boxers of all time is Muhammad Ali. Ali had the crowds on his side in ways like no other boxer before him, and no one since. Facing off with him was also facing off with the crowd.

There would be no neutral territory anywhere on the planet when fighting Ali. It made for nights when fighters with superior skills would fail miserably because he had the show to go along with his solid boxing skills, and amazing physical conditioning. Butch, Bobby, and all the guys at the West End Gym aspired to that. Butch had that kind of potential. He was a solid boxer, had a fantastic combination, could switch styles, and there was a family legacy in the Gloves. He also had a built in fan base, thanks to the success of his older brother.

The next fight for Butch would be just a few weeks later on November 19, 1982. That fight would end with Butch as the victor but not in any way he really wanted.

This fight was stopped in the second round when his opponent, Dave Casetti, was disqualified. One newspaper article said that the referee, Tinker Picot, stopping the fight was a huge series of favors to everyone involved.

It was said to be a favor to Butch because of the way his opponent was approaching the fight. Throughout the first round Dave would just come up and get Butch into a clinch, then quickly raise his head and head butt him in the face. This could have, and soon would have; caused a huge cut on Butch's face and that would have ended the fight immediately and not in Christokos' favor.

It was a favor to Dave because it saved him from Butch. The man was obviously out of his league and would have been beaten badly, perhaps injured, if the fight had been allowed to go on.

He did everyone in the arena that night a favor. For the first time ever a fight involving a Christakos was on the verge of becoming boring. That would just not do.

After the fight, the ever level headed Butch merely said that he would have to learn how to fight a guy like that.

He had no real regrets, and merely took it as a learning event. That type of learning was necessary for someone with a future in the sport.

According to many boxers, it can be done. You can fight a guy like this. You merely have to keep your distance and depend on jabs, but that wasn't Butch's or the typical Christakos style. They liked it up close and personal.

The only other thing Butch would say about that fight is that he didn't want that victory. He wanted to prove he was the better boxer and he would not get that chance. It didn't matter, Butch's fighting spirit was still intact and he was ready for the Nationals.

The Nationals were held in December of that year. That night was a huge disappointment for the younger Christakos.

He lost that fight but not by being KO'd or by some decision. In the first round, of the first fight in the tournament, he was hit hard in the head. He was ready to continue to fight but there was a cut inside his mouth that needed medical attention.

Butch argued with the referee and said that he could go on. He wanted to finish the fight. He was taken from the arena to a hospital and it took 20 stitches to close the cut. Butch wanted to stay in the ring.

That kind of fighting spirit is what comes from Lowell. It is what has driven this Nation for over two centuries. The spirit of our men and women to overcome the odds and continue to work despite any problems to achieve the goals we have set for ourselves.

Butch would end his boxing career as an amateur but would rake in three Golden Glove victories in his weight class bringing the eventual family total to eight.

Later in life Butch suffered from weight problems and died of a heart attack in his forties but he fought until the end. He was a loving father and husband.

The picture above is Butch Christakos when he was fighting in the Golden Gloves. He and Bobby really pushed each other to be better in, and out, of the ring. That is what families should do, help each other strive to achieve.

Chapter Four
A Fighting Town is Born

Many New England towns have a long history, and oftentimes the residents are more than happy to tell the entire story to visitors. Lowell Massachusetts (the center of town is shown in the picture above) has been a somewhat organized town since before the United States was a group of British Colonies. It was also the first large-scale factory town in the country, and as a result, is considered to be the birthplace of the American Industrial Revolution.

How did Lowell obtain that distinction?

The first people known to have settled in the area now known as Lowell were the Pennacook Indians. This tribe was a part of what is known as the Wabanaki Confederacy. Due to their location, and the landing point of the original European colonists, they were one of the first tribes to interact with these new Americans. As a direct result, they were unfortunately stricken with many diseases that these original settlers inadvertently transmitted to this peaceful tribe, causing many of them to die as a result. The Native Americans had no immunities built up against European diseases as the new inhabitants had built these immunities up across a lifetime.

This tribe of Native Americans were also, unfortunately, raided on a regular basis by other, more warlike Indian tribes such as the Mohawk and Micmac Indians. This directly contributed to their numbers dwindling even further.

These native peoples were primarily farmers and generally stayed out, as much as they could, from the intertribal wars that would go on throughout the region. Their participation in any of the conflicts, including those that went on between the Europeans, was limited to selling food and various supplies. They were merchants, entrepreneurs, and generally speaking, not hostile by nature.

The Pennacook Indians had a unique form of government for the time period. It was largely democratic, or in other words, they voted for their leaders, instead of having leadership passed down through the bloodline of some ruling family.

There had been historic examples of democracies in Greece and Rome, but that was the stuff of history books. This was democracy in action and it could be observed first-hand instead of only seeing it as words on a page.

Some historians believe that it is this tribe of Indians that taught the colonists the potential virtues of this type of government.

Lowell is a town that should be honored for what it has given us. It doesn't just give us boxers, or textiles, but it may have given us some of the bedrock ideals our Nation's founders chose to build a form of government around.

As can be seen from the story of these Native Americans, Lowell is a fighting town, these earliest people, from what is now Lowell, fought for survival. They may not have survived but the town did. Their spirit lives on in the citizens of the region to this day.

During pre-colonial, and even into the colonial period, many goods were shipped by boat or barge across waterways. In addition, farming, and irrigation for those farms, also requires access to waterways. Back then there would not have been irrigation systems like we have today involving pumping water from some distant location to where it is needed. A more natural solution was needed.

In order to irrigate crops the natural flow of the river would have been used to access the water needed to grow larger quantities of food. Prior to this type of irrigation of crops Indian Tribes could only gather things that happened to grow naturally. The use of waterways greatly increased yields and allowed for organized farming. This use of rivers for this type of task dates back many centuries, but was used here to find a place that a group of Native Americans could settle down and spend generations in one place. It allowed enough food so that their numbers could grow without famine setting in, something that was common in the hunter gatherers that existed prior to this type of irrigation.

So, you see, Lowell grew organically. Later on its expansion was thought out, and planned, but early on it just happened due to nature deciding that reasonable farming land along with running water would allow people to survive.

As we said, the city is located about twenty five miles northwest of Boston along the rapids of the Merrimack River. This is the river that would allow the easy irrigation of the early farmland as well as provide easy movement of various crops to market.

Textile Mills line up along the Merrimack River.
PHOTO: Tom Duggan, Special Thank you to Helicopter Pilot Steven Reel of North Andover Flight Academy.

****

Later these same rapids would allow for powering of the industrial and textile plants in the area, as their construction predates electricity. These plants would have been powered by water turning giant wheels, which would then turn the machines to do that manufacturing.

So you see, it was no accident that Lowell ended up where it was. It was necessary in order for this scrappy little town to survive. First people had to fight the water to get it to do what they wanted for their economic survival.

In other words, the people in this town have been tough from the start.

The town underwent a transition in the 18th century. That is when the first mills were built. The initial industrialists build two, these were a sawmill and a gristmill. Sawmills were necessary in this area because of all of the timber being harvested from local forests. Gristmills were necessary for grinding grain.

At this point in history it was far more economical to process the raw materials near their point of origin than to ship them long distances. Today, thanks to modern transportation, the production of raw material and the processing can be in two completely different locations without causing massive increases in cost, which would then be passed on to consumers.

All of this building, construction, and shipping made for a tough group of people living in Lowell. It really set the stage for the blue collar roots of the town. These tough folks had to fight against everything, including the Pawtucket Falls.

It turns out that the river has a series of waterfalls, right near where it passes what is now Lowell. These are great for powering the mills, but terrible as a shipping lane. Water will speed up right before them, making the plant water wheels turn faster, and more predictably. But, at the same time, it is impossible to move goods down a waterfall, especially with this one being 32 feet tall.

What is a fighting town to do?

Merely walk the goods down river from one side of the waterfalls to the other?

Were they going to load them on wagons and have horses, or oxen pull them?

How would you get boats to the other side of those same falls?

There had to be a better way for a blue-collar town with a fighting spirit to handle this.

Lowell found a better way. In 1792 a group that would come to be known as the Proprietors of Locks and Canals Association was formed. They set about construction and the eventual completion of a canal to bypass these waterfalls in 1797. It took them five years of hard work, but it paid off. They now had a waterway to get their goods to market, one that didn't involve offloading and reloading them. This gave direct shipping capabilities to the Atlantic Ocean in Newburyport.

As the saying goes, no good deed ever goes unpunished.

By this point the town that would become Lowell had competition in the local area. Another series of canals were built known as the Middlesex Canals allowing for direct access to Boston. Lowell would have to first send their good to Newburyport, and then on to Boston. This really limited the economic viability and desire to use the Pawtucket Canals versus the competition, and they fell to the point where they were almost not used.

The town was not to be stopped; one bad round would never keep them down.

In 1810 a man by the name of Francis Cabot Lowell went to visit Great Britain. He was an American by birth and was a businessman by trade, who happened to specialize in the production of textiles. When he went to see how Britain businesses dealt with the manufacturing of these goods he found that British had a great system, but their law completely prohibited the export of their machines. They wanted to protect their competitive advantage in various fields.

It didn't matter, he found a better way, and he fought the law and won. He didn't break any laws (Bobby, do you hear us, don't break the law again), we want to stress that. He found a loophole.

He memorized the designs and when he came back to North America he built, essentially, the same machines. He even found one or two improvements. Remember, this was before patent law so technically he didn't do anything wrong. He was perhaps unethical, but he didn't technically break the law. It may have been creative, it may have been sneaky, but it worked, and was legal.

When he returned in 1813 he organized the Boston

Manufacturing Company and built a cotton mill in a town somewhat to the south of Lowell, called Waltham. Today Waltham is home to many corporate headquarters and is one of the more affluent towns in the area. Perhaps that is historically the case as the manufacturing town was centered there, administratively, with operations in other portions of the local area.

This mill was one of the first in North America to use power looms (powered by water) rather than looms powered by the feet of the human workers. Waltham drew this power from the Charles River that eventually runs through Boston and passes places such as Fenway Park and MIT.

Francis Lowell died in 1817 and a man named Patrick Jackson succeeded him in the business. Jackson was having so much success in the business that he needed a second plant. He decided that placing that plant near those falls and the canals of the Merrimack River would be the ideal location.

The result of that decision was that Jackson would start a new partnership known as the Merrimack Manufacturing Company. They broke ground on a new mill in either 1821 or 1822 and completed their first product run in 1823. This early product coming out the door was refined cotton. They found success almost immediately and soon the need for more mills was obvious. The town had fought, and won.

It was going to grow.

After this growth started going gangbusters they decided to split the town off of what was then Chelmsford and named it after Mr. Francis Lowell.

This happened in 1826 when the population had reached a whopping 2,500. Within a decade the town had grown to 18,000.

The town had fought for survival and done so well in this particular round that on April 1, 1836 it was chartered as a city. That was done by an official title grant from the Massachusetts General Court. Lowell was the third city to be officially organized, and recognized, in the state of Massachusetts.

This new found size and official recognition led to the opening of museums, theaters, courts, jails, and anything else you find in a city...including entertainment. Early boxing matches started to appear around this time.

They didn't fight by today's rules, these were bare-knuckle boxers, but the need for entertainment was there, and as we said, many of the citizens of Lowell have always loved a good fight.

By the time the mid 1800s had arrived Lowell had grown even more. It had lots of new mills, a canal system that was over five miles long, and over ten thousand workers. These canals supplied the workers with power through the movement of water, and that water was giving them over ten thousand horsepower to work with at any given point in time, day or night. These workers were now producing fifty thousand miles of cloth every year. This was all done without electricity.

Not a bad way to put up a fight for survival!

Now that Lowell appeared to be on the verge of victory, and being declared a champion, fortunes turned for our little city. The American Civil War began.

This was not great news for a town where the economy is based on cotton. Virtually all of the cotton they were processing was coming from producers in the southern United States. For cotton, it turned out, that processing was so cheap in the mills of Lowell it was worth the shipping costs. As a result of the war, they couldn't get raw cotton anymore and their raw material stockpiles were now worth more than the finished product.

Many of the mills (those based on cotton) were now virtually unused, and unemployment in the town rose...again. This was only a temporary situation as many of those who lost their job went to serve in the military, many never to return.

After the war the mills roared back to life. Because of all of the men who did not return companies had to recruit from all over the region. The new employees included women, mainly widows, to work in the manufacturing plants. This allowed the city to win another fight, and come back in this latest round in the never ending fight for survival and eventual prosperity.

By the 1920s, however, life had changed again. The New England textile industry was in disarray and production began to migrate to the South. When Lowell first obtained all of this business the only technology available to power the mills was rivers and waterways.

By the 1920s that was no longer true, as coal powered plants were now dominant in providing power. This allowed entrepreneurs near where the cotton and other materials were produced could now do the job without concern or cost of having to ship the material halfway across the country.

It appeared the Great Depression would find its start in the same place as the American Industrial Revolution. Lowell was going to get knocked down hard in this round and unemployment was very high. It stayed that way until World War II brought life back into a city that had 40% of its residents on government assistance. The reprieve would be short lived, and when the war needs (mainly parachutes) ended, so did this uptick in jobs.

Lowell would continue to bottom out until the 1970s, but that is for a future chapter. Below is a photo of Lowell's city hall in 2014, a building that dates back a long way and has been witness to the unfolding of much of this Nation's history.

Lowell City Hall and Police Station. Photo: Larry Richardson, 2014.

Chapter Five
Lowell Hits the Canvas

Being a book about boxing it is important to understand that nobody, ever, ever, ever, wins them all. Lowell, being a huge boxing town, was destined to lose a round or two. But, as the old saying goes, what doesn't kill us, makes us stronger.

Had the town not undergone so many ups and downs over the years perhaps they would not have been able to find so many talented and willing boxers among the local population.

After World War II many of the mills and manufacturing plants that had roared back to life to support the war effort that would ultimately defeat Hitler, once again fell on hard times. These plants shut down, again. As a result, so did the economy in large portions of Lowell.

Starting in the early 1950s with the decline of these manufacturing jobs until the 1970s when Wang Computer decided to place some of their research labs in town everything was falling apart. There was ever-rising unemployment, and where there are no jobs, and desperation, there is always rising crime. This rising crime eventually led to organized crime in the form of the mobsters involved in various rackets around town. Some of these rackets were fairly simple and predictable, while others were far more dangerous.

Illegal gambling places were common, mobsters the likes of Whitey Bulger could be seen on the streets, murders happened regularly, and very little positive could be seen going on. The city needed a between-rounds pep talk that could get them back in the fight for prosperity, and they needed to do it right away.

Things were in fact, so bad that the now Greek Acre achieved a first in the nation status that no town would want. They received the first ever grant of money to perform a Federal Urban Renewal project. What this did was provide funding to level many buildings that were vacant, or in various stages of foreclosure. They did this to build newer, more useful buildings in their place or, in some instances, to allow fewer places for homeless drug addicts to hide and get high.

In the 1960s one of the very things that helped build the town, met its end. The Merrimack Manufacturing Company's mill yards and boarding houses were demolished. They were replaced with some warehouses and public housing projects. This is not exactly a direct replacement that would provide jobs. Instead it provided places for people on government assistance to sit and wait for their check and hope for a better life, or at least some means of employment to come to town.

This wasn't the only post World War 2 challenge facing Lowell as it was face down, with its eyes closed, on the canvas, being counted out. Many of the theaters left, the department stores were all gone, and only a few smaller specialty stores remained. There were a few cafés, coffee shops, and the odd barber shop but nothing of real note. Overall there was really no industry to speak of other than retail stores in which you could spend your government assistance check.

Many of the buildings making up what there was of the skyline were torn down to be replaced by parking lots. We aren't sure what people were going to be parking to go do, but there seemed to be a large number of these lots being built. With the industry leaving and nothing else really downtown one can only wonder. But, by this point the Golden Gloves were centered in Lowell, so perhaps it was for the rabid boxing fans to come and watch?

It didn't seem that Lowell's leadership of the day had any long term plans to get to the next round. It seemed like they were ready to throw in the towel.

With the increase in crime, especially organized crime, there was an increase in buildings being burned to the ground by arsonists. Many of these were insurance ploys or just someone looking for something to do on a weekend, but multi-alarm fires were commonplace.

Many of these buildings that were burned down were never replaced. The prevailing wisdom would be that people took their insurance settlements and left town to start over someplace else.

Around this same time some of the taller buildings underwent a massive transformation. Property tax and upkeep on a building will be much higher if a building has many floors. Some owners, in an attempt to save money, and stay in Lowell, had a few of the top floors removed. This was an attempt to reduce their cost of ownership. Sometimes that would work sometimes...not so much.

Throughout this time the downtown area started to

look old and rundown. In an attempt at making the town look less "old New England" some of the buildings were given a facelift. The owners would typically put some modernized façade to make the place look new, but rarely were upgrades done on the inside, so it was all for show. In a business, as in a boxing sense, that rarely works, and certainly didn't in this case. All show and no go makes for a short fight.

The city management then got involved in what should be done to help the business environment in town to thrive. Their version of "help" was to widen some of the roads which destroyed some of the more convenient parking spaces that customers would use to get to those few businesses that remained. Now customers would have to go to the larger "pay to park" lots and walk to the businesses in order to do whatever it was they came into town to do.

This practice resulted in increased costs of doing business for consumers. Anyone who has been in business will tell you that with increasing costs comes a decrease in customers. That isn't really the growth model the town was seeking for their business environment.

In a few cases it was even worse. The structures some businesses depended upon were destroyed by these new road lanes. For example, there was more than one gas station that lost the ability to fill its underground tanks thanks to these new lanes. Those businesses shut down as the cost to redo their facility proved too much of a kidney punch to their bottom line.

This was not limited to gas stations or filling tanks. If

a single building contained many businesses on its first floor, or some of the mechanical structures the building depending upon were too close to the road when it was widened, these structures were destroyed.

More than one newspaper article, or resident, described what remained of the city as something out of Europe during World War II. The overall condition, and the state of decay of what had been such a vibrant city, really a beacon of industrial strength for the region, was so bad that some residents started talking about raising money to declare parts of downtown "historic zones" and try to restore these buildings with some sort of historical preservation funds. It was either that or let them be condemned due to lack of maintenance.

Some of that took place and actually still exists today with, for instance, the Textile Museum, among other things in the downtown area.

Before the museums of today there were entire regions of the town controlled by the mob. In the early days the mob would clean up town and stop crimes faster than the police. The only crimes they wanted to see happen were the crimes they were committing. As a result they didn't want cops in their neighborhoods because of some unrelated activity. That was just an unnecessary risk. In fact, there were several areas of Lowell where, if you committed a crime without a mobster's permission, you had better hope the police found you first.

That is, unless the cop who responded was on the payroll of a mobster, then you were in double trouble.

This was back when protection money really kept you

safe from petty criminals. These were the classic organized crime groups that might do illegal things, but would do it because it was their business. If you paid them protection money you could assume your business was safe. Then the organized crime started to change, a lot, and then you were paying protection money to protect yourself from them. Protection still wasn't a guarantee if you had something they wanted.

This was a time when most mobsters refused to deal in hard drugs. This also shifted, and soon mobsters preferred to deal in whatever was most profitable without regard to anything other than money, and that was usually drugs.

This, less honorable, type of organized crime, was the mafia of Whitey Bulger. Whitey was (actually still is) one of the most notorious, feared, and for a long time sought organized crime figures in the history of the United States. For a many years he remained in hiding and on the FBI top ten list but back then he was walking free.

Whitey was so confident in his ability to stay free at one point he had a price on a Boston reporter's (Howie Carr) life because Howie was the only one doing investigative reporting on the Boston mob. Howie is just fine, he still does a radio show and writes true crime books, including one about Mr. Bulger and his brother William.

Whitey started his criminal career as a teenager way back in the early 1940s. He first appeared on the public radar when he was arrested and charged with larceny. By this point he was a member of a street gang that called themselves The Shamrocks. He continued with a variety of smaller crimes until he, for some reason, joined the US Air Force. While on active duty he was sent to the stockade (jail in military lingo) for multiple assaults. Once out of the stockade he went AWOL (Absent With Out Leave), but it didn't matter he wasn't going to make a career of the military anyway. He was eventually discharged (honorably) in 1952 and headed back to the Boston area.

There are many questions surrounding Whitey and his involvement with various government organizations.

Was he an informer for the FBI at this point?

Was he involved with the CIA?

Both are likely true, and that is the subject of many other books. One of those books, as we mentioned, is by Howie Carr and called The Brothers Bulger. It's a good read if you are interested in the subject.

One thing is for certain. While he was in prison he got involved with a CIA program called MK-ULTRA. This program had a goal of developing mind control drugs. As a result, for a year and a half Bulger, and other inmates, were given, among other drugs, LSD. The CIA was messing around with brain control and they had a theory about using drugs to achieve the goal. We assume it didn't work, but that organization isn't one that would return our calls with questions.

He was transferred from his prison in Atlanta to one more fitting of his type of high profile criminal. He went to Alcatraz in 1959. There he made friends with some other people of like criminal mind and formed partnerships that would last until long after his release in 1965.

Once out of prison Bulger went to work as a bookmaker and loan shark.

What else is a man with his skillset to do?

He was a very large, and growing, figure in the Irish mob in South Boston by 1970.

By the late 1970s there was a consolidation of organized crime groups in the Boston area. Bulger, along with a man name Flemmi, took over what was left of the Winter Hill Gang. Around that same time the FBI was getting pretty aggressive at locking up mobsters which left a huge power vacuum for Whitey to step right into.

He was nothing if not a creative genius as a criminal. He even found a way to win the state lottery once and get a share of a $14,000,000 jackpot!

In his peak years, which were throughout the 1980s, he had his fingers in a very large number of criminal enterprises. He had an empire that had influence all over Eastern Massachusetts. He was into extortion, loansharking, bookmaking, truck hijacking, arms trafficking, drug dealing, and anything else he needed including murder for hire.

He was eventually caught and found guilty of 19 murders.

Humorously to those of us that live here Massachusetts is home to many corrupt politicians. It is interesting to note that Whitey Bulger is the brother of former President of the Massachusetts Senate Billy Bulger. We aren't saying that Billy was corrupt or even a criminal but...he did have a criminal in the family.

Now, Billy was also relatively shady in a variety of ways. It is true that he was the longest running President of the Massachusetts Senate. He served in that elected body for eighteen years. He was also the President of the University of Massachusetts. He was forced to resign from the position in 2003. It turns out there was a Congressional hearing about and they were asking questions about any communications he may, or may not, have had with his then fugitive brother. He refused to testify.

During the hearing Billy was asked what he thought his brother Whitey did for a living.

Think about this for a second. His brother appeared to have no job but had income and was suspected of many things.

His brother, the politician must have had ideas. But his answer was interesting.

Billy Bulger said in testimony, "I had the feeling he was in the business of gaming...whatever. It was vague to me but I didn't think for a long while he had some jobs but ultimately it was clear that he was not being, you know, he wasn't doing what I'd like him to do."

He was relatively vague on purpose. Anything more specific and he may have been investigated for conspiracy, or worse. He was forced out of his position by then Governor of Massachusetts Mitt Romney, and did not get his University pension.

Whitey had a constituency of a different sort, with a reach from Boston to Lowell and far beyond. Now what does this have to do with Boxing? Really not much except for the fact that the Golden Gloves were in Lowell, and had been for many years by this point. In order to organize some of the fight cards the mob had its fingers into that as a part of their business. They had to have something for people to bet on. Boxing was certainly part of that.

When researching this book we saw a large number of pictures of people preparing for fight night. Often times these included the organizers of the night. Looking at the photos you cannot help but notice one or two cousins of known organized crime members involved in putting the night together. Every boxer interviewed for this book said they never fixed a fight and they never took a dive. Looking at the boxers and their weight classes at the time, anyone would notice that there were some real mismatches put on some of the cards. We are going to venture out on a not so shaky limb and say that these mismatches were to encourage the sucker bet and make their night of gambling more profitable.

Most of the fighters we met would never back down form a challenge. Many would view a mismatch as a way to prove themselves. Every once in a while one of the fighters would beat the odds, but more often than not, whoever was taking the bets would make a ton of cash.

Things in the fighting world are much better organized today, but it is worth noting that casinos do host a large number of boxing events. Apparently some things just won't ever change.

The takeaway to this is that Lowell, Massachusetts was indeed a rough town that has had its ups and downs. Its ups are great, they are euphoric in fact. Its downs, however, are really far down, perhaps like a really hard knockdown, for lack of a better term.

When the Golden Gloves were in the heyday, and Lowell was producing thirty or more professional fighters at once, it was certainly a low point for the city but a great high for boxing. The sport, was so popular because, among many other reasons, people needed an escape. Spending time in the boxing gym meant you weren't spending time off the streets. It meant you had a chance at a better life, not a chance at a better prison cell.

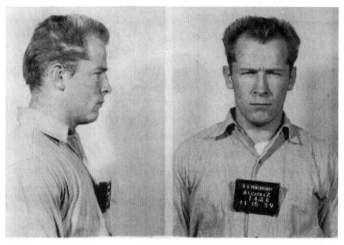

This was Whitey Bulger as he was transferred into Alcatraz. Whitey is currently in Federal custody where he will remain for the rest of his natural life.

Chapter Six

Focusing of Energy

Bobby was, and still is, a relatively rambunctious guy. As any parent can tell you finding ways to focus the energy of a child like that tends to be a full-time challenge.

In researching this book there were a large number of people who graciously gave up some of their time to be interviewed. Those ranged from ex-sparring partners, people he fought in the silver mittens, several Golden Gloves opponents, a sister, an elementary school teacher, newspaper reporters and even one barber who cut his, and his father's hair, for decades.

For anyone researching a town, or an individual, always talk to a local barber. Those guys that have been in the same place for decades will know all of the dirt on everyone. On the same note, be careful what you tell your barber, they will share those things with anyone willing to ask questions. There is no barber client privilege such as the one enjoyed with lawyers or therapists.

One thing about Bobby Christakos has rung true amongst every one of those conversations. He is a fighter at heart. He fought in the ring, he fights outside the ring for things he believes in, he fights with people when he works as an umpire for various baseball organizations, and he even started a fight or two when he played a little organized basketball. He has also been in a fight or two in bars, such as at The Cosmo in Lowell that resulted in his arrest on five different occasions. He even met his wife in that same bar, and we are sure that she and he have also had a fight or two over the years as a married couple.

Two of those instances of fighting spirit stand out among the rest. They stand out and demonstrate that this man, as a kid, could have gone either way. He could have ended up in prison, or as a role model. His father, and his involvement in boxing kept him out of prison for years, and may have saved his life. Once he left the boxing world he again headed down a not so great pathway. That was when he met his wife and cleaned up his life.

The solutions for many problems in life are to have something, or someone in your life you are passionate about. When he, and many others, don't have a passion for anything or anyone in particular, things generally turn bad. Many women out there are fantastic at keeping their husbands in line, and Bobby's wife deserves accolades (Maybe a Golden Glove of her own) for keeping him out of trouble for decades.

The first was the one previously mentioned way back in chapter one. When Bobby was a teenager he was sitting in his father's coffee shop, that was really a bookie joint in disguise, he got into a verbal argument with a kid a few (two or so) years older than him. That doesn't sound like a big difference when you are an adult but, the difference between a fourteen and a sixteen your old male are reasonably significant.

The argument occurred inside that coffee shop. That coffee shop, as we mentioned, was in Lowell's Acre. The Acre was not a place where you could get by on just talking smack, you had to stand up for yourself.

The argument went something along the lines of one of the kid's insults the others father, those insults escalate one at a time until finally someone (ok it was Bobby) said something along the lines like "Now, I'm going to kick your ass."

Well, what gets left out of the newspaper articles that have mentioned this incident, but Bobby's sister will confirm, is that the older kid walked outside (literally) and waited for Bobby. This fight has been mentioned many times in articles that were written about our boxer and it always seems to just say that Bobby got into a fight, we assume they were quoting Bob. We dug just a little deeper. It turns out his mouth may have written a check that his fists just couldn't cash. That is not something you do in the Acre without, eventually, getting yourself into deep trouble.

Bob, not being stupid and realizing he was physically way outmatched, sat inside the coffee shop. His father looked at him and told him to "go finish it, you can't be all talk."

His father was close by and would stop things before they got too bad but wanted to teach his son a lesson. It was important in the Acre, and hell in life really, to not talk yourself into a corner, which Bob had just done in dramatic style. It was a lesson that today's parents would not teach in this fashion, but this was the 1970s not the 2010s. The world was different. It was better in some ways and not nearly as good in others.

Bobby, knowing not to cross his father, went outside. Needless to say he got his butt kicked. Put another way, he got his ass handed to him. Not badly enough to need a doctor but it was bad enough that the bruises were remembered. Bob's father was the one that shoved him into the West End Gym run by Art Ramalho. Art immediately put Bob to work learning the craft of boxing.

Art, on many occasions, has said that Bob was a guy who loved to brawl. If it was done in the ring, it got that out of the boy's system. If it was done on the streets, it would be out of his system but his safety, well, that might be another story. He would be in trouble soon enough, and likely never again have a future that didn't involve a cage.

As it was he came very close to that cage on more than one occasion.

That fight wasn't the last he would get into outside the ring, but it was when things started turning around for him, for the time being. He would have other peaks and valleys throughout his life but this was a time when he was certainly on the upswing. He did still have to learn a bit more of wrong from right but when he fought it was always for the right reasons (with one or two possible exceptions, but no one is perfect).

Think about it like the great nation we live in. No one likes their nation to get into a fight. No one really wants us to get into a War. These things do from time to time happen. We would like to think it is always for the right reasons. They usually are, historically there may have been one or two that weren't, but America has always been reluctant to go to war.

One of Bob's teachers from junior high school showed up to his birthday party in 2014.

The teacher told a story of another "outside of the

boxing ring" fight, but even she agreed it was a fight for the right reasons.

There was, shortly after he started learning how to box in junior high, an event in a class Bobby was in. There was a classmate of his mouthing off to the teacher who tried to calm down the out of control child. The mouthing off was much worse than a typical teenager being a jackass. The teacher tried the traditional methods of trying to defuse the situation with no luck as the student continued to escalate every chance he got.

Bob, being Bob, in his typical direct fashion, took matters into his own hands. He, and the mouthy student left the room under Bob's "urging" to talk about how one should respect adults and shut up (we are paraphrasing this part in an effort to clean out the expletives that were used) so everyone else could learn.

The teacher seemed to be shocked to this day, some three and a half decades later. But that is the kind of person Bob is.

In this case the teacher recalls that a few minutes later the mouthy student, along with Bobby, came back in the room. Bob, slightly ruffed up, the mouthy kid, really ruffed up. The student then apologized profusely for his behavior.

It would be hard to imagine today that things would go the same way. Even if a student sided with the teacher there aren't many places where this story would go the same way. Even if it did both kids would be in an enormous amount of trouble. There would have been trips to the office, parents called, and possible expulsions for both, and who knows what else. One thing is certain, the story would have not ended with the two coming back in the room and sitting down. Does that mean we do things better or worse now? It is a tough call.

When asked, Bobby did say he did what he had to do and that was about it. He really wouldn't say much more about it. The teacher beamed with pride when she told the story. She even said that she did not bring the incident up to his father during a parent teacher conference as she didn't want him to get into any kind of trouble.

Did he do the right thing?

Well, the outcome was what would be the desired conclusion but perhaps it could have been handled differently. Perhaps if he had learned early on that this is not the way things are handled outside the boxing ring there may not have been as many arrests for disorderly conduct or bar fights later in life? Who knows, but one thing is certain, he achieved his goal and the end was the right thing for the class full of students to be able to learn.

Even today, Bobby Christakos works with kids through his umpiring of little league to help some of those kids have a better start in life, to help them end up in a better place. He tries diligently to teach them right from wrong. He also will not give them an inch. They either make the play, or they don't. There are no freebies.

Now, to get back into the boxing gym, Art said that from the start he was a hard worker. It was said by the coach and by those around him that he trained harder and more often than just about anyone else. Even today, if you are looking for Bobby, when he isn't at work, you will most likely find him exercising at the Lowell, YMCA.

Back then, he was in the gym seven days a week. He hit the weights, he ran, he hit the heavy bag, he did everything a boxer preparing for a chance at a title fight would do…and he was only in the Silver Mittens. He wasn't even old enough to be in the Golden Gloves yet.

He was prepared, but he hadn't had a chance to prove himself in a tournament yet. That time would come, but not for some years.

After about a year he was getting pretty good at boxing. He was getting pretty good at knowing how to take a hit, and how to hit back.

Well, that was when he ran into that kid that pummeled him outside his father's coffee shop. Bob, might have picked a fight. Perhaps it was not the right way to handle things but this was The Acre in the 1970s. The Acre is much different now.

Bob said something to the kid like "hey you remember me you….." That kid yelled at him and said he could kick his ass again and that Bob should 'walk away.'

Bob has never been someone to back away from a challenge and this was no exception. Round two of this went much different. Bob walked away without a mark on him.

The other kid however looked much as Bob did on the first round. Bob stood up for what he thought was right, now in this case it might have been better to walk away, but it was what he believed to be the right thing to do at the time.

His energies over the years have become better focused, and he has stopped fighting for such silly reasons as he lost once. However, kids are kids, and Bob is much older and somewhat wiser now.

He will still step to the plate to protect someone if he had to, and does still have an amazing uppercut, but he is much more focused now on understanding the right time and place for everything, largely thanks to his wife, Debra.

Chapter Seven

Lowell Gets an Upgrade – Wang Computers

Bobby Christakos' career as an amateur boxer really started to get moving in the late 1970s when he was given a spot on the team, and a trip to the National Golden Glove Tournament. New England was not going to be sending someone in his weight class due to another boxer dropping out so, Bob was given a huge shot to compete at a level that could really show that he was capable of competing with fighters well beyond his experience level.

But before that happened Lowell had to win a fight for the future of the city.

Lowell, like Bobby, was taking a few hits around that time. But, in another close parallel, they were both putting some numbers into the win column.

At the time Lowell was in a ton of trouble. Unemployment was high, crime was on the rise, no new jobs were on the horizon, and many buildings were empty with no new tenants to be found. With the textile industry on the ropes and no sign of any kind of manufacturing in the near future, Lowell found some help in the form of a growing local Massachusetts company known as Wang Computers.

Wang was a very early computer company that began as a University spinout in the 1950s. It was originally in Cambridge, Massachusetts until it grew to the point that made it impractical to keep the entire company in the bustling downtown area. At that point Wang moved much of the company's operation north of

Cambridge to Tewksbury, Massachusetts in the 1960s and ultimately relocated again to Lowell in order to find cheaper rent as a cost savings measure in the 1970s.

In the 1980s Wang was in its heyday and Bobby Christakos was hitting the peak of his boxing career.

In the 1980's Lowell was reaping many of the benefits of Wang's growth. At one point the company was worth $3 Billion and had a worldwide workforce of over 30,000 employees.

Wang made very effective use of the blue collar skills found in Lowell for many years. These skilled laborers were put to work building Wang products and maintaining the machines that made up the assembly lines of their manufacturing interests.

Many of the skills were slightly different than the traditional textile industry experience that was common in Lowell in the previous decades. This was electronics, this was the future. This was something people gladly did a little retraining to be part of. This was also the start of a great turnaround for the city at the very same time Bobby Christakos was really starting to rock and roll in the boxing ring.

Wang's first set of products were typesetters, of a sort. The first product was known as Linasec. It was a specialty purpose computer. It mechanically moved paper of various types of machines generally known as Linotype machines. This allowed for printing to be done in a much more automated method than ever before.

Linotype machines were used in printing of things like newspapers, magazines and larger format posters like one would find in movie theaters, or outside a the Golden Gloves tournaments. These machines were used from the 1960s and well into the 1970s until they were replaced with a newer technology.

That is always the way of the world, once a technology proves to be useful or profitable someone will come along and make an improvement or make it obsolete. That is why companies like Wang have large research and development departments. It is far better to be the person that makes your product obsolete than to let someone else bring the replacement to market.

These machines would produce an entire line of type written material at once. That doesn't seem like much today, but it was a huge leap forward then.

It would use metal characters to do this (much like a manual typewriter only faster). These would be used when thousands of something needed to be produced in a short period of time. Think of them like the copy machines of the past.

These machines replaced an industry standard where humans would manually set type letter by letter, a technique that had been used, in various forms, since before the time of the Revolutionary War. It was a giant cost saver for the companies that did this type of work. It also served to bring the prices of these items, newspapers and magazines for instance down dramatically, which in turn makes them more widely available to consumers.

In its day, the machine was a giant leap forward and it really allowed newspaper publishing to enter a new era. Essentially, it allowed a very small number of operators to type set the pages of an entire newspaper every single day instead of the giant teams that were required prior to this. Before this type of machine only huge companies (such as the New York Times) would have the ability to produce a daily product. Essentially this type of technology broke apart the monopoly held by these larger companies.

Prior to the linotype invention (which was in 1884 for an early primitive mechanical version but perfected by Wang), no daily newspaper had more than eight pages.

Why bring all this up in a book about a boxer or a town full of them?

Prior to this, Lowell was an economic mess looking for a way to employ its workforce of blue collar workers. Wang came in, gave the town a between rounds pep talk, and brought them back from an almost certain knockout.

As we shall see Wang computers, for years, also fought against obsolescence problems that would push it to the brink and then eventually bring themselves back through some creative technology. They also fought off some larger opponents, such as IBM, to stay in Lowell for a long time offering the town an economic boost it so desperately needed.

Once the Linasec was replaced by some superior technology, Wang exited the industry and entered into other, more high tech computerized products. Their next huge money maker was calculators.

Imagine that, in the backdrop of Lowell becoming a boxing haven for the entire East Coast, with Bobby winning by knockout after knockout, it was also, once again, leading an industrial recovery for the region. All the while Bob was living in a rough and tumble neighborhood of the Lowell Acre.

These calculators, for their time, were revolutionary. They knocked the competition right out of the ring. Remember this was the 1960s and 1970s. Wang had built, and was manufacturing, what was probably the first ever calculator that could fit on a single desktop, and available to consumers at a price they could afford. Before their product line this type of technology could only be seen in scientific research laboratories.

The point is that at the time this sort of thing was unique. These calculators, and the manufacturing of them, brought even more jobs back to the region, they brought stability back to Lowell and they brought new skills into the city looking for a future. The city, and Wang computers fought through another tough round and came out the victor.

The first customers for these were scientists who hadn't built some sort of a one-of-a-kind machine for themselves and, of course, engineers. After a few years the customer set expanded to include the financial industry.

There is even one famous case involving Wang's calculator getting the company into a fight. This was when the calculator was put up against a mortgage table that had been used by the industry for a long time. The challenge was that there was a mismatch between the calculator output and the mortgage table. In the end, after careful examination, the calculator turned out to be correct. Wang won the fight.

Wang computers certainly decided on the right place to put their business.

In the 1970s, especially the second half of that decade, Lowell was once again home to a revolution of sorts.

In this case it was the introduction of another innovative product from Wang computers. This time it was the word processor. Before this revolutionary new product anyone who wanted a typewritten document anywhere in the world would have to use a typewriter. The most common of which was the IBM Selectric. This is hard to imagine today in a world of the internet, laptop computers that cost less than $300 and cloud storage, but back then it was amazing. Everyone in business wanted one of these machines.

No longer would memos have to be redone every single time, contracts could be saved for future reference. It really was a HUGE timesaver. As the old saying goes, time is money, and this thing saved people time.

Chalk another win up for the Wang Corporation!

The Wang original word processor had a storage capacity on a single storage tape (this predated disk drives and way predated USB memory sticks) of approximately twenty pages. It was a new day dawning for technology. The original introduction of these word processors was in the early 1970s, otherwise known as roughly the time Bobby was getting beaten up outside his Dad's coffee shop, and dragging people out of classrooms so that everyone else could learn.

This was just the start of another growth period for

Lowell. It was the same time period where things were turning around for Bobby. A new day was dawning for everyone.

Wang had journeyed from calculators to word processors and was about to enter the full-up personal computer business. In the late 1970s and early 1980s most consumers still wondered why anyone would need a computer at home. Now everyone has multiple computers and wonders how we could survive without them.

These computers were some of the earliest desktop systems. The Mill City was well on its way to becoming a beacon of hope for the technology industry of the Eastern United States. Everything from Boston to Lowell could have been the Silicon Valley of the East Coast (if only our winters weren't so harsh). The region had led the world in textiles and it was possible they could lead the world in other ways.

Wang Computers' first foray into these new market was a minicomputer that would do some amount of data processing. This was another leap forward over their word processors. Now people in the financial industry, for instance, could calculate loan rates, show investors rates of return, and all at the click of a few keys. It first hit the market in 1973. It was so early on that very few people in the world had ever seen an actual computer much less used one. At that point the closest anyone had come was an episode of Star Trek.

In 1977 these computers had really progressed into something usable by a much larger group of consumers, and would lead to intense growth in Wang as it was starting to compete more directly with

IBM in its core business. They came out with their new Wang VS Computer Line. These would put them in the same business as the IBM 360 and in fact their system was compatible with the IBM 360 series system software.

These systems could be programmed in a number of different computer languages, many of which are not used today but, at the time were cutting edge.

The CEO of Wang computers, a Doctor An Wang very much wanted to compete against IBM. IBM was already a World Champion in the computer industry. Wang wanted a title shot.

They had been beaten up by the larger company over some patent arguments concerning magnetic storage devices used in their earlier product line. Wang had some victories but really wanted to take on the larger company on across as many fronts as possible.

The only challenge was that Wang was never taken all that seriously as a computer company. They were generally regarded as "the adding machine guys." In other words, Lowell would remain a semi-pro in the computer industry.

There were many great boxers in Lowell, some not so great, others really bad. Well, Wang did breathe life back into Lowell, but suffered from one fatal flaw. When its founder passed away the company quickly lost its ability to attract new business. It filed for bankruptcy in 1992 and never recovered.

Fortunately, Lowell had recovered a bit by then. One of the many interesting things about large technology companies is they tend to spawn other companies around them to provide them various forms of support.

They also tend to have employees that want to continue their education. These employees are everywhere from the blue collar manufacturing type common in Lowell, to more white collar research types doing new product development. This caused Lowell to greatly expand the local University campus.

University of Massachusetts' North Campus, Photo: Tom Duggan Special Thank you to Pilot Steven Reel of North Andover Flight Academy.

****

University of Massachusetts at Lowell had grown a bit and become a research institution in the region. For students who couldn't afford to pay the tuition or perhaps couldn't meet the admission standards at MIT or some of the other Ivy League school in the area, UMass Lowell offers an amazing education and really is very under-rated. Massachusetts has more than MIT and Harvard (Doctor Wang, the founder of the company was a Harvard Professor).

UMass Lowell has continued to grow and today has taken over a large part of the city. It has brought stability to the area and helped to bring the town back just a bit.

Just like a boxer who had to train, and retrain to become professional, Lowell has had to train, and retrain the local workforce to do what is necessary to win.

In the coming chapters we will dive deep into Bobby's boxing career. There will be more knockdowns to come, but for the most part Lowell has survived, as has Bobby.

In boxing many fighters look for what is called a tune up fight. That was Lowell. It was the tune up town. It was where you went when you were down and need to build confidence with an easy win.

Lowell is no longer the fighter you go up against on your way to a bigger and better fight, now Lowell is a pro. That pro brings employment to the area and even the Acre is no longer as rough as it once was. There is even an arena known as the Tsongas Center where they host everything from concerts to sporting events. The city has really turned itself around and become a Champion.

Chapter Eight

The 1977 National Golden Gloves

New England has always had an exciting series of tournaments for the Golden Gloves. There are local favorites, new fighters, old fighters, favored referees, disliked referees, excitement, nervousness, you name it and this tournament has it. What all of the participants are hoping to win isn't just some local notoriety, or their name in the paper, it is a trip to the National Golden Gloves.

In 1977 the Nationals were held in Hawaii. No fewer than three hundred fighters from thirty two cities around the United States all went to Oahu in search of their very own National Title. If you could pull in that National Victory then perhaps you had a shot at the professional ranks and some real money.

That year the headliner from the New England team was going to be Jim McNally. He had been fighting in the tournament for a number of years and this was his shot at a big victory. He was twenty two and a senior at Northeastern University. He had no intention of turning pro, so this was his last chance, and he was the heavy weight entry for the team.

That year New England sent a number of fighters to participate in the nationals. They included the following:

- Paul Defayette (112-lbs)
- Dominic "Pepper" Roach (119-lbs)

- Joe Phillips (125-lbs)
- Dan Avery (132-lbs)
- Bobby Christakos (139-lbs)
- Wilber Cameron (147-lbs)
- Matt Maybry (165-lbs)
- Jim McNally (178-lbs)

As an interesting side note; Jim went on to have a really interesting career. As of the fall of 2014 he just retired from the United States Secret Service where he had been on the protection detail of several US Presidents including George HW Bush, Bill Clinton, George W Bush, and Barack Obama. He even worked on a case where they seized millions of dollars in counterfeit money. This was back when the service was part of the Department of Treasury. Since that time it has become part of the Department of Homeland Security.

Jim has moved back to the Boston area since retiring. He now runs a boxing gym out of North Reading Massachusetts. On the next page Bobby can be seen hitting the speed bag at the grand opening of Jim's Gym.

This may have been Jim's last tournament, but he did have a very impressive amateur career. His win-loss record isn't the most interesting bit, and statistics are what they are. According to a conversation with him, one of the thrills of his time in the ring is that he would train and get picked for some interesting duty from time to time. When training for a big fight the professional boxers will look to the amateurs to find sparring partners. Jim was a gifted amateur, and a big guy.

Those two things combined to make him one of the favored sparring partners of Marvin Hagler when he was training for a big fight. He was able to keep up with Hagler for a few rounds, but the professional fighters are used to much longer bouts, going into a larger number of rounds than the amateurs. As a result there would always be a few of the guys from the Golden Gloves picked for the pros to train with. But, Jim was one of the favorites. He wouldn't hold back and could always make them sweat. He was, and to this day is, no pushover.

Jim, as it turned out, was the roommate of Bobby during that national tournament. At the time Bobby was 17 and a high school junior at Lowell Voke which is the nickname for The Greater Lowell Technical High School.

This is a special school in the area. It was founded in the late 1960s as the Lowell Trade School. This is where you would go if you had no intention of going to college and wanted to explore other options. Today the school prides itself on continuing the tradition of the various trades but also getting students ready should they decide later to go the college route in life.

The school offers education in a variety of trades. They include such things as:

- Carpentry
- Automotive Technology
- Machine Technology
- Metal Fabrication
- Small Engine Repair
- Masonry/Bricklaying
- And many more…

The school fits with the general employment of the town. Some fantastic tradesmen are amongst their graduates, even today. Some fantastic fighters have walked those very halls.

The vocational school also has a very active athletics program. While they don't offer boxing (what school besides a college could for liability reasons) they do offer a multitude of other sports. One of those is basketball. It turns out that Bob was a member of the basketball team, on top of his activity in boxing.

His hard work (or hard headedness depending on how you look at it) also came into play on the basketball court. Remember Bobby is not a very tall guy, not typical of what you would picture on a basketball team. For instance one of the authors of this book, (Tim) is six foot three inches tall. Below a picture can be seen of Tim and Bobby over at Jim McNalley's gym. By the way Tim sucks at basketball, by his own admission. He enjoys it but is terrible, never put him on your team.

According to several people he was exciting to watch. Remember that athletic events such as basketball or boxing depend on a fan base. If the fans aren't engaged or enjoying themselves they won't come back. Bobby never forgot that. He would do things that would get them excited. He would engage with the fans in any way possible.

But, it was more than that. When he started playing he was terrible. He stunk as much as any short guy can stink. But, he was not to be deterred. He stuck with it. He practiced. He would repeat outside shots, three point attempts, free throws, and he would stay there for hours practicing every day.

With practice he got better and eventually was able to make a three pointer like no other short guy could.

All of this activity in basketball helped his boxing

career as well.

One thing boxers depend on is stamina. With Bobby spending five days a week after school and weekends in the West End Gym improving his boxing his time on the basketball court helped him improve that stamina. All of the running really paid off. It helped improve his reaction time and reflexes. It was also the type of activity not a lot of boxers spent their time doing, so perhaps this gave him an edge over some of the other folks in the Golden Gloves. It certainly didn't hurt. Especially at that national tournament in 1977.

Initially, Bobby was not supposed to be a member of the National Golden Glove team. But, when someone dropped out it left an opening for a fighter in his weight class and the honor went to Bobby Christakos to fill that slot.

Here he was, he had been boxing for only two years and, all of the sudden he was on his way to the nationals, and with very little warning. He found out two weeks before that he was going to get on an airplane and go fight in Hawaii. At this point in his life he had never been further away from Boston than New York City which is only a few hours train ride from his home in Lowell.

For anyone not from the Boston area, Hawaii is not only geographically a long trip but you probably would be hard pressed to find two places less alike. Hawaii is laid back, it is relaxed, it is sunny, and filled with warm weather. Boston on the other hand…not so much on the laid back, and as for the rest, Bobby felt very much like a fish out of water. It had to add to his nerves. He was already the underdog and the mental game had begun.

He may have been the underdog but to quote Art Ramalho from a 1977 Lowell Sun Article by Rick Harrison titled **Lowell Slugger, Christakos Could be Gloves Surprise**, *"I wouldn't sell him short. He's a walk and hand type of fighter. He loves to mix it up inside, and we've been teaching him to go underneath more for this tournament. He is the most dedicated hard working kid we have."*

Remember that boxing is more than just a physical matchup…the mental game matters. He was already very out of his comfort zone geographically and probably distracted as well, given the social scene in Hawaii, as he was a very young man at the time.

That same article has a quote from Bobby that shows how, even at this early age, he was in control of the mental game as well as the physical. Bobby said, *"I know for some of the boxers that the trip itself is a big thing. But I've been given this chance and I really want to make the best of it."*

Bobby was not expected to advance. Other members of the team were really thought to be the real contenders. However, Bobby was the only person to advance past the initial fight of the tournament.

His first fight was against a boxer named Herb Scurles.

He didn't win by knockout, but he did win a solid decision. He took a lot of hits throughout the three round fight, but he had a fighting style like Joe Frazier. He was a real bulldog, he was relentless. He never let up until pulled back by a referee, or his opponent went down.

After the fight Bob stood in the ring not really knowing what way the decision was going to go. He was nervous, and was thinking that the judges were taking too long. Then, suddenly the decision came. He heard his name called as the winner and he admits it took him a moment to realize they were talking about him.

The first reporter he saw asked him what he thought of the decision and he said, *"Apparently aggressiveness really counts here and that's good for me."*

Bobby was still catching his breath at the time. It took him a while to get his mind in order. It was still spinning with the euphoria of being at the nationals, taking all those blows, and getting a victory. It was a big deal for him, as it would be for anyone.

After having caught up with reality there were a few reporters that traveled from the continental United States along with the teams to Hawaii.

The Lowell Sun had a member of their staff there to cover the match. After regaining his composure Bobby was reported to have said,

"I started working to the body in the second round, which is what I try to do in every fight. It takes a lot out of him, and he told me when we both came to lie down after the bout that he was really tired in the second."

Bobby did advance to the quarterfinals and, was the only member of the New England team to advance at all. Unfortunately, in his next fight he ran into the man that would eventually win in his weight class.

Bob had his first taste of victory. He did not win, but he would be back.

The winners from that year's tournament were:

- 112 lbs – Orlando Maldonado, from Miami
- 119 lbs – Wayne Lynumn, from Chicago
- 125 lbs – Bernard Taylor, from Knoxville
- 132 lbs – Samuel Ayala, from Fort Worth
- 139 lbs – Thomas Hearns from Detroit
- 147 lbs – Michael McCallum from Miami
- 156 lbs – Curtis Parker from Pennsylvania
- 165 lbs – Keith Broom from Knoxville
- 178 lbs – Rick Jester from Detroit

New England may not have had a winner that year but we would be back. Lowell, and New England never back down from a fight.

Chapter Nine

There can be only one, or can there be?

Other than paying homage to the awesome 1980s movie starring Sean Connery and Christopher Lambert called *The Highlander*, why have we decided to name this chapter "There can be only one or can there be?"

After his performance in the national Golden Gloves tournament the previous year, Bobby Christokos was taken much more seriously as a boxer. There was a lot of buzz. All of the typical questions were being asked.

Would he eventually go pro?

Would he just end up to be another kid from Lowell who had a shot and blew it?

Would he end up strung out on drugs?

Was it just luck?

Funny thing about people who work hard, dedicate themselves to something, and have some talent. They get lucky a lot.

Does the sarcasm come through loud and clear? We hope so.

After the nationals Bobby was improving his skills. He redoubled his efforts. He exercised more, he conditioned harder, and fewer people were willing to get in the sparring ring with him.

That last bit is amazing considering he was working

at the West End Gym and its long list of professional and semi-pro fighters that called it a home at that point in time.

One of the other guys at the West End Gym was a Lowell resident by the name of Jim Leary. Jim Leary really wanted to fight Bobby. He didn't want to spar with him; he didn't want a practice round, he wanted this one to count.

Recall that back in chapter two we explained the sport of boxing and all of the different weight classes. Jim Leary was the same weight class as Lowell's Bobby Christakos. The two were competing in the Golden Gloves and it was just assumed that someday they would collide at a tournament.

What else made this a unique matchup?

If you recall back in that same chapter two we introduced various styles of boxing. Bobby, as we know was a brawler. Jim Leary was also a brawler. Brawlers have no finesse. They lumber around the ring ready and able to take hits all day long and deliver very few, yet very powerful punches. These are knockout guys.

Neither of these men was fast on their feet. The most important thing a brawler has going for him (if he is going to go very far) are a huge amount of power and a really hard chin. They need to be able to absorb huge amounts of damage. A fight between these two would be the rough equivalent of two dump trucks playing a game of chicken. Put another way, it was like they were two trucks of the same type in a demolition derby.

If you have never heard of a demolition derby, don't

worry we are somewhat showing our age by mentioning them as they are rare these days. For those of you reading this who are not old farts like us these events sometimes happen at county fairs and festivals. The rules of the event are pretty loose but the concept is simple (and a picture can be seen below).

A group of people, typically five or more, get in their cars. They drive around an arena smashing into each other as hard as they can. The last driver with a car that is operational (and we use that term loosely) wins. That was what these two fighting each other was like. They both had a style that said take the hits, and dish out slightly more than you take, just make sure the ones you give out really count.

Both of them trained harder for this fight than for anything they had done before. Perhaps the hardest part of preparing for this fight was that they were both in that infamous, and unique West End Gym training under Art Ramahlo.

One of the things that a fighter does in preparation for a fight is to study the style of their future opponent. Usually that is done through film, or watching them compete here or there. In this case they could easily just look across the room and see the other guy. They could know everything about the other guy, strengths and weaknesses, stamina and speed.

That wasn't what either of them wanted and both agreed that they should train separately. In fact, they avoided one another as much as they could. If one of them was in the gym the other would leave. They were firewalled from each other.

But it still posed problems as both fighters were learning from the same master. They were the same style of fighter. They were both dedicated. This was going to be an interesting matchup.

When they weighed in on fight night they both weighed 147 pounds. This was going to be a rumble. This would be six minutes (three rounds two minutes each) that had the potential to be remembered for a very long time by anyone who was there that night.

Fight night came. Nerves were frayed, hearts were pounding, and no one in either corner had any idea what was going to happen once that bell rang.

The two men were introduced, they were sent to their respective corners with instructions, and the opening bell rang.

They came toward one another, with no finesse; they

lumbered toward the center of the ring like Roman Gladiators.

The first few seconds the men were looking for an opening. They gave up looking and started swinging.

No one knows who landed that first punch it happened so fast. It hardly matters. The two men were so evenly matched it hardly mattered as they could both take a hit so well the first punch was irrelevant.

The fans watching that night said it was less than thirty seconds in before it resembled two guys who said some nasty stuff about each other's moms.

Through two long rounds they pounded one another over and over. Anyone else in their weight class would have been down on the mat before the end of the first round. There were some lethal combinations that caused the crowd to gasp, and wince, then gasp some more on more than one occasion. Somewhere in that crowd was probably a doctor that wanted to rush to the ringside and help one or both of them.

The funny thing was that these brawlers. They kept taking the hits and neither of them showed any hint of slowing down, no hint of being in any kind of pain and no hint of stopping.

That is, until the end of that second round.

Both men, sweaty and bruised, walked slowly back to the corner. They sat down and could barely lift their arms. Their corner teams looked at them and gave the typical pep talk but these guys were tired.

The blows to the body had been vicious. Four minutes of punishment dished out by someone of the same style, someone the same weight, someone who had learned the craft from the same trainers.

It was to be expected that this would be a close fight. It was exhausting. The men came back out for the third round, and this is where the fight would be decided.

Sweat was hitting the canvas. Blood was coming from cuts all over their faces. Everyone in the arena thought they would both fall from exhaustion before the end of the fight. Perhaps there would be two guys on the mat being counted out. No one could be certain how they were still standing or how it would end.

Christakos would go to the body; his body would also take punishment. No one wanted to go down. This was a pure test of wills. Each one was iron.

As expected for most brawlers, this fight would go to the end of the final round and decided by the judges. The two men stood, slumped over in the middle of that ring waiting to hear the decision. Both of them were certain that this could be a tie.

In fact, had this not been a decision to see who would advance to the New England Golden Gloves from the Greater Lowell tournament, and from there, if successful, to the nationals, it may very well have been a tie.

Bobby was the winner. After they announced his name the crowd cheered, some gasped, others disagreed. Bob had his hands raised in the victory stance as happy as he could have been in his career.

Those hands rose slowly but they rose. He had won the test of wills. He had worked hard and that hard work had paid off. There would be only one winner from the West End Gym and it was Bob. The blue collar boxer had won another one.

When they left the ring, both needing physical assistance, both men went to a room in the back and out of the public eye to rest. They had no other choice, it was rest or fall down.

In the typical after-bout interview that takes place after every fight Bob said, "Once we were in the ring, for three rounds, we're in there to kill each other. After that, we're friends again."

That sums up the crew that boxed at the West End Gym. They took their sport seriously and would never hesitate once in a fight that counted. They fought to win. Bookies didn't matter, friendship didn't matter, and even family relation didn't matter once that opening bell was sounded.

This wasn't the end for these two men.

***

In February of 1978 there was a rematch. This was another Golden Gloves fight to the finish.

This time, they knew each other's style better. They had been in the ring together and walked away bashed and battered. They were again, evenly matched, both stubborn as mules and both claiming to be in the best shape of their lives.

The fight took place in front of a crowd of 3,500 people. It was a night to remember. They all knew from the last time these two met that neither would go down; they were too stubborn for that. They would beat on each other until the final bell, and then perhaps they would both fall to the mat, but not before.

There was only one difference this time. The last time they met both men had been fresh and ready to go. This time Bobby had fought just twenty four hours prior, meaning he was anything but fresh. That served to be a major disadvantage.

From the moment the bell rang memories of that first fight went through the heads of both men. It was the same fight all over again. Neither men would make the same mistake as last time and covered their body without fail.

So what is the opponent to do when this happens?

They went after one another in the head from the opening seconds. Pounding in the face without mercy. This went on and on for two rounds.

Christakos would pound Leary in the head in much the same way as IBM would pound Wang Computers with lawsuits trying to keep its stranglehold on certain bits of technology.

Leary would beat Christakos in the head in much the same way as Wang would beat the giant company in court.

Bobby was losing. He was tired. He knew it.

Late in the final round he came back with a huge left that stunned Leary to his core. Leary staggered but did not go down.

Bobby had him on the ropes but he was so tired he couldn't take full advantage of the stun while Leary remained on his feet and began to recover.

Then, the final bell rang, and the two men who really were friends outside the ring leaned on one another for support. They were superior sportsmen who stayed in the ring to the last second of the final round.

The Lowell Sun had a fantastic article reporting the details of the fight; here is what each had to say after the fight, which was a decision for Leary meaning their record fighting one another was now tied at one each.

Leary said, *"I planned to pressure him, knowing he had to fight last night, to try to tire him out. But he didn't get tired. He is in tremendous condition. He trains seriously and is always in tip top shape."*

Leary tried to catch his breath before the second sentence could come out.

"The start of the third I had him against the ropes for just a second, I was giving him my best shots but he just stood there. It was frustrating."

Bob, never at a loss for words, to this day says he would have won had he not fought the night before, but on fight night back in 1978 had this to say, *"It wasn't a matter of catching the punches or getting tired. It was the idea of having two fights back to back. Last night hurt me. I couldn't throw to the body he stayed too close to me. That's why I went to the head, and lost."*

Chapter Ten

He's a Masshole, but he's our Masshole

If you are reading this and you not from New England, we have to explain a few things.

First and foremost, living in Boston and the surrounding towns is a different world as compared to some parts of the United States. The further north one travels into New England the more you will find that there is a totally different breed of person living here.

We have a saying for people we like that are well…kind of assholes. We call them Massholes. You know. Your friends, maybe your family has people in this category.

One of the people involved in putting this book together has not always lived in the area (Tim Imholt). However for years, because of his job, he had an office at The Massachusetts Institute of Technology (also known as MIT, you know that place where all the Wicked Smaht kids hang out). Before that he worked at or with several other Universities around the United States in a variety of capacities.

As we continue to say throughout this book, the spirit of one Bobby Christakos is the spirit of Lowell, and in many ways it is the spirit that ignited a revolution back in the 1700s that eventually won this country the freedom to self-govern.

So what do we mean by different?

If you visit New York City, which Bostonians will say is not New England, but some will say is the entry

122

point to the region, you will find something that shifts as you go further north. The city has neighborhoods. Those neighborhoods have things like Wall Street, China Town, Manhattan, the Arts districts, etc. People that hang out in one or the other have a tendency to not cross lines on a regular basis and have multitudes of friends, or even parties with people from the other neighborhoods.

For instance, when the New York Yankees (or Mets depending upon your neighborhood) are on television one can easily find sports bars that are showing the game. One will rarely find someone who works on Wall Street or at New York University as a professor sitting next to someone from Brooklyn cheering for the same team enjoying a beer together. We are not saying there is anything wrong with that it is just what happens.

Let's go north into Boston.

When the Red Sox are on...the world is a much different place. One can routinely find an MIT Professor next to a construction worker just absolutely not caring about who does what for a living. The team is on; everyone wants to be in a sports bar CLOSE to the Fenway. Nothing else matters but the team. Period. It is being a fan that matters; there is no separation of social classes. Famous author Stephen King is known to have season tickets (not in a luxury box) and can be seen walking around the neighborhood before a game, that is how far this goes.

Another interesting thing about Boston and most points in New England further north.

You don't fit in until you are willing to behave in specific ways. For instance, Tim says he first felt like he was starting to fit in well when he was walking across MIT with a Professor and they had to cross a busy street. A taxi came careening around a corner and almost hit the pair of them. Tim and the Professor could be heard screaming obscenities at the cab driver with equal quickness and volume. THAT is New England. We are rough around the edges. We are politically correct in ways, and very much not in others.

In New England towns you will often find they are places where you can look at a friend you ran into at a bar, and say "Hey asshole, what are you doing here? Let me buy you a beer."

How far does this go? Well, there is a fantastic comedian, actor, and director named Denis Leary. He is from one of Boston's surrounding cities called Worcester. That town is not pronounced how you think it is from the spelling so don't try it, unless you are from around there, then you know.

He wrote, recorded, and made famous a song as part of his standup comedy act. That song is called "I'm an Asshole."

It is laugh out loud funny. Check it out on YouTube if you haven't seen it. Then send him a note through Twitter, Facebook or his website and call him...well, an asshole. He'll be fine with it.

So does anyone really care we call each other names, and are relatively nonpolitically correct most of the time?

No one will care about the asshole part. We mean no

serious offense buy it…It's just the way things work around here, for the most part.

There is an area of Cambridge known as Harvard University where they take PC to a level no human ever should. Even those of us from here pick on those guys so don't lump us in with them.

Tim also says that upon becoming an official New Englander being brutally honest with your friends about their flaws has been taken to an art form.

So, that brings us to Bobby Christakos.

He is true New England. He epitomizes the rough around the edges never say die fighting spirit that allowed the Red Sox to come back from a shut out series, we can have no points going into the end of the game against the New York Yankees, come back and not only win that game but go forward to the World Series and win. We like a good fight that much.

How much of this type of New Englander is Bobby?

When doing research we called Bob and asked him if he knew this other boxer we wanted to talk to…Bob's response was poetic.

"Yeah I know that retahded fuckah."

We left the accent in just for fun.

He meant no offense to anyone, and he got us to that boxer who referred to him as a "dickhead."

In short, he's an asshole, but he's our asshole, so it's ok that we call him that, but don't *you* dare do that or there will be a fight.

In 1979 Bob was in the Golden Gloves and a variety

of other amateur non-tournament related fights. There was one in particular that was a very controversial victory by decision against another home-town kid named Jimmy Sheerin.

After the fight they stood in the center of the ring waiting for the announcement to come. They announcer started reading the results.

Remember that the judges look for very technical things when scoring a fight. They are also sitting closer than the crowd, they are typically experienced fighters, and none of them (hopefully) have been drinking, unlike the fans.

Now, Bob has always been a fan favorite. He knew that putting on a good show was part of what makes for a successful boxing career, and packing in an arena. But, this night, none of that mattered. The crowd was behind the other hometown favorite Jimmy who, they thought, fought better.

They announced Bob the winner.

There are things said by the announcer after the winner is declared but no one could hear any of it. The boos, and remember this is New England, other far less polite things started coming toward the fighters. Some projectiles, empty beer, somewhat empty beer, food, hot dogs, anything that could be thrown started coming at Bobby, some went towards the judges … It was like 'to hell with the judges we have our opinion and screw yours.' That IS New England.

But the audience reaction didn't matter; remember from chapter two that the judges rule the ring. The decision stood.

In truth, Bobby Christakos was behind on points all night. Only in that last half minute did Christakos come on strong with a flurry of combinations, jabs, hooks, and anything else he could. It was like he had a burst of energy you see at the very beginning of a fight but rarely in the final seconds. To the judges, that was enough for Bobby to win on points, despite being behind for more than two rounds.

The crowd didn't care.

Remember back when we said that New England has rabid boxing fans?

New Englanders also have VERY long memories; they hold a grudge for a long time. This was just the start of booing Bobby Christakos. Those boos came anytime he would walk into the arena there in Lowell for the rest of his boxing career. But hey, it was along the lines of "Hey asshole we remember now let me buy you a beer."

For instance, let's fast forward to the Golden Gloves tournament in 1979.

Bob walked into the Lowell Auditorium to fight in front of a sold out crowd. He was about as welcome as an out of town fighter who walked up and told the Lowell crowd that Manhattan Clam Chowder is the only real Chowder.

First, anyone from Boston knows the correct pronunciation is Chowdah, but that is another story. If you have ever visited here you know we take Chowdah very seriously. It never ever comes from a can and it certainly isn't from Manhattan.

This was the semi-finals of the New England Gloves

Tournament. Bobby Christakos should have been treated like a sports god. By all conventional wisdom, he should have been cheered for from the moment he walked in until the end of the fight. After all, this was his home town.

None of that mattered. He walked into the ring, and was jeered. But remember, this is Boston and the surrounding area, and he's our bud, so no problem, right?

Once the fight started, however, Bobby came out pummeling his opponent from the opening bell. The hometown crowd, in mid jeer fell silent for a moment as Bobby punched away, and then instantly forgot their hometown feud, put it all aside and cheered wildly Bobby Christakos.

Many said afterward that they were angry about the decision and they really wanted to remind Bobby that nobody gets a free pass. It doesn't mean we hate you, it means we think you screwed up and you are going to hear about. Nothing personal, but you're an asshole.

They didn't seem to care that Bobby just shows up and fights, he doesn't decide who wins. Bobby said he couldn't understand why there were taking it out on him, if it's a bad decision they should be taking it out on the judges, not him. Well, not here. But the hate was fleeting as Bobby once again outperformed to some cheers despite the fickle fans that called him an asshole at the start of the fight.

Bob lost that night to Marlon Starlon, but he put on such an amazing show the spectators still talk about it today. There were times when the crowd was on their feet after an amazing combination. Bob could always make them cheer. But this was the start of a love/hate relationship.

When asked about it in 1979 Bob said, "My father warned me this was going to happen. But it don't make it any easier. This should never happen to a fighter from Lowell at home."

Bob's own father wondered if half of the crowd knew why they booed, or it was just some sort of herd mentality.

In the end, the crowd cheered for him, they did love to see him fight, but this is New England, so we, of course, have to remind him that he is an asshole, but he is our asshole.

Chapter Eleven

Class, No Style, Victories Leading to the Pros

When talking to folks around Lowell everyone who called The Acre home seems to have a story about Bobby Christakos. Some flattering, some not so flattering, some were downright insulting. One thing rang true through every conversation, people had made up their minds whether they loved or hated Bobby Christakos and very little was going to change that.

As we heard in the previous chapter, Bobby can be, well, an asshole. This is common among gregarious and successful people in Massachusetts, so much so that, as we alluded to, there's a word for assholes from Massachusetts. Masshole.

Bobby was a textbook Masshole. And like most Massholes he had a certain degree of class.

A Masshole with Class? How can that be?

When Bobby was very active in the Golden Gloves from 1977 - 1982 he used to go jogging every morning.

In every boxing movie, and every boxer we spoke to says that a part of his/her exercise routine is running some number of miles every day. Rocky, The Fighter, The Champ, Ali, all these movies have scenes of boxers running long distances to train but most of them never explain why. After all, there is no long distance running in a boxing ring.

So what's the point? Just to lose weight or get in

shape? All that time boxers train with jump ropes and punching heavy bags would achieve the same goal.

Boxers spend a lot of time running because it's the easiest way to increase your aerobic fitness. You need substantial aerobic conditioning to survive twelve rounds. If you are not very fit, you can slow down for a bit, get some rest, recover and get back in the game, but the more fit you are the less recovery time you need. This longer period of rest requirement is great if you are a quarterback playing football and the defense is on the field for a while, or if you play baseball there's a lot of time to rest between plays. But, in boxing you don't get tens of minutes off to rest and catch your breath, you get one minute…no more, no less.

If you are in excellent aerobic condition and you do a lot of running, you can recover in that one minute between rounds and come back with more energy than your opponent if he is not as aerobically fit.

The owner of one of the local stores reached out to us when she heard we were writing a book about "Bobby the boxer" (her words). She owned a store in downtown Lowell that did embroidery. Her store used to embroider many of the boxing trunks for the guys in the Golden Gloves. Some would request their names or nicknames or the names of their girlfriends on them. Bobby's were simple. He would simply want "Christakos." He wasn't boxing to win the heart of a girlfriend, he was there to win and that was it.

Every morning Bobby would be jogging by the woman's store which was not in the best part of town.

Bobby knew that neighborhood, and he knew the

street criminals who preyed on women, and small businesses. They all knew who he was, and most of them were deathly afraid of being on his bad side.

Concerned for her safety, Bobby made sure to work her neighborhood into his jogging route every morning and jogged in place outside her store chatting with her as she went from the car to the store.

Once he knew she was safely inside he would go on his way and finish his jogging route. If she was late, he would wait for her. That was class.

Bobby barely knew the woman well enough to say hello, but he was concerned for her safety and he knew that by doing this every day the "bums" in that neighborhood would get the message. It was simple, don't mess with this lady or you will deal with me.

Asked about his morning jog, Bobby grunted and said "Men look after women. It is just what you do."

We are cleaning up the language a bit but you get the point. Too often today, if someone sees a commotion or a crime going on people's gut reaction is to take a photo with their cell phone and be "first" upload it on social media and then maybe dial 911. It's much rarer today to see someone step up to the plate and do something. Bobby is still the guy that steps up to the plate.

Did Bobby's sense of class extend to the boxing ring? After all he was a brawler so that can't be true, can it?

In early 1981 Jeff Northrup penned an article for the Lowell Sun entitled "Christakos, No Stylist But the Man Has Class."

In that article he points out that many people have

accused Bob of being stylistic. He was a brutal fighter and his matches were ugly. He loped around the ring like a Neanderthal. To watch, and evaluate his style, he didn't really look like he had much talent, but once the punches started you could tell that he did. The same was true for his sort of class, but he had that too.

In early 1981, Bobby was fighting in the Golden Gloves Tournament and won what can only be described as a decision that the crowd, well, just did not agree with in any form or fashion. They started booing Bobby Christakos, he left the ring as a victor but then went to talk with the tournament organizers.

He told them that he would pull out to make the fans happy, if that was what it took to keep them happy with the tournament. He liked the crowd on his side, and he didn't want the Golden Gloves to have trouble filling the arena because of him.

He wanted to win, but he wanted to win clean. He did not want to be a smear on the reputation of the tournament, or the organization.

That is class. That epitomizes the spirit of most citizens of Lowell, Massachusetts.

After much discussion, Bobby continued in the tournament. He went forward to fight Terry Crowley who, at the time, no one had ever heard of in connection with boxing.

Another win for Bobby, after which trainer Art Ramahlo said, "I wish I had a gym full just like him. The kid don't want to lose. Nothing fancy. He trains hard and he's got a lot of heart."

Bobby throws himself into things with passion. If he

is protecting a woman from a robbery that may never happen, it didn't matter. He was committed. He had class, and continued to give the crowd his best. He didn't care if they disliked him personally as long as they liked the show he put on for them and respected his talent and hard work.

THE LAST AMATEUR YEAR

Throughout his entire boxing career Bobby was nothing if not consistent. He showed the class we discussed, he was competitive and trained as hard as anyone. 1982 was going to be his year. This was his last year as an amateur and after this he was intending to turn pro. It was an exciting time.

The type of class, dedication, and ability to entertain a crowd could carry him far as a professional fighter. It is the type of reputation that boxers long for, yet few achieve. The greats have it, the not so greats want it. Bobby had it.

In an article published on Jan 10, 1982, Dennis Whitton (now the Sports Editor at the Lowell Sun) wrote an article about Christakos called "He Lives for Boxing," summarizing the situation quite well. We will summarize Dennis' article here.

This was going to be his year. He had trained harder, he was better mentally prepared, and the tough times were going to be behind him. After all, this tournament would be his stepping stone to the pros and hopefully, the big money.

In his article, Whitton even said that, "just five years ago Bobby was in a fight outside his Dad's coffee shop that led him to boxing."

He also pointed out that he had been a daily visitor to the West End Gym, almost without a break, throughout those five years. At the time, people said you couldn't chase him out of the place, even when they wanted to turn off the lights.

In this article Dennis also pointed out something that is a point of pride for Bobby, even today.

When he first showed up at the gym he was getting his head punched in every single day. In less than a year it was Bobby doing the punching and very few boxers wanted to get in the ring with him, even if it was just to spar.

There were a lot of fighters at the gym, how could this be? Surely someone besides his brother would get in there and help Bobby train.

Bob is so competitive that even when sparring he didn't pull a punch. He hit just as hard as if he was in the last round of a championship fight. He didn't let up. He would knock people down and taunt them like a real fight.

That could be positive or negative depending upon your perspective, but it certainly helped him to win during the actual tournaments.

He had life all figured out. He was going to win this tournament then turn professional with a manager named Petronelli in Brockton. Petronelli, at the time, was managing Marvin Hagler who was the World Middleweight Champion. The future was certainly looking up for this kid from the Lowell Acre.

Bobby assumed he would do better in the professional

ranks because there were more rounds in the pros and he usually got a slow start in all of his fights. He had the stamina and he knew longer rounds would tire his opponent while he was just catching his second wind.

Former World Boxing Champion Micky Ward and former Golden Glove heavyweight Jim McNally both agreed that yes, in the Golden Gloves, Bobby had issues with starting slow.

However, there is a huge difference between being conditioned for three rounds and being able to last twelve. Both said they weren't as convinced that Bob's fighting style as a brawler, which by definition includes getting hit a lot, would serve him well in the pros. If he could switch up styles then maybe, but that was something he hadn't shown to be very good at up until that year.

That being said, in the Golden Gloves tournaments Bobby was notorious for losing the first round then coming from behind, sometimes a few precious seconds before the final bell. It was the kind of comeback that always made for a good show, and brought the crowd to their feet.

Most Golden Gloves boxers have a tendency to tire after two rounds (something Bobby capitalized on perfectly in his career). Professionals don't tire so easily.

The Whitton article in the Lowell Sun was written before he was competing in that year's tournament. To quote Bobby about the upcoming competition he said, "All I have on my mind is boxing…No drinking, no girls, no nothing. This is it."

His daily workout routine in preparation for that

year's tournament was rigid. Every single day, seven days a week, he would go for a three mile run, do four rounds of shadow boxing, three rounds on the heavy bag, fifteen minutes of skipping rope, fifty sit-ups, thirty pushups, and then he would spar with his brother.

That is a rough day for anyone. In 1981, partially because of all the hard work, people were calling Bobby Christakos the blue collar boxer.

His reputation was that of a guy unafraid to work hard in and out of the ring. He was striving to improve every minute of every day. When asked about his singular style of boxing being pure brawling and how that might hurt his chances Bobby replied, "It is kind of hard to change your style, although my father is trying to make me more of a boxer. I'm moving my feet a lot more now, boxing a lot more. Hey if I have to bang to win I'll do it, but if I can outbox a guy I will."

So he appeared willing to listen and change things up if he had to. Dennis Whitton added, "It's really hard to imagine Bobby dancing around the ring. He is a classic brawler. Take two give one. That kind of fight is always one the Gloves fans love to see."

Finally, Dennis asked him if he expected to be booed when he walked into the ring, something of a Lowell tradition at that point, he said, "They'll probably do it this year too," with a roll of his eyes.

GOLDEN GLOVES OPEN FINALS

In the open finals of the Lowell Sun Golden Gloves

of 1982, Bobby was set to fight Joe Feeney. At this point Bob was the defending Lowell Champion.

From the second of the opening bell of the first round, Bobby went on the attack. Usually when this happens, his opponents, (all amateurs themselves and unsure if they will ever go further), look for a rock to hide under. Joe was a different kind of fighter. He was smart, and he knew Bobby's style.

Joe didn't run and hide in the corners. He knew that Bobby did this; he knew Bobby was a brawler, and he was ready for anything that Bobby could dish out. Joe met every single Christakos rush with a quick jab to the head, scoring points, then moving. It was a brilliant performance for an amateur. This worked well for the initial part of the first round, and was a large part of what helped Joe go the distance.

Bobby was ready with a few surprises of his own. He knew he was going to have to adapt and change up his style with anyone he was up against, and Joe was just another fight. When he quickly figured out what Joe was doing he adjusted, stepped up his game and caught Joe by surprise.

Putting Bobby the Brawler in the back of his mind, he tried boxing a bit. He danced a little, stunning the crowd, he moved around and he made the defensive moves regular "Brawler" fans were just not used to seeing.

Although he started the first round behind on points, Bobby did come back to win the first round by a small margin. But he was tired.

In between rounds the people in his corner helped him figure out what to do next.

In that second round Feeney tried the jab but Bobby got inside and managed to turn it into a brawl. He was back to true form, catching Feeney off guard yet again as he has just not adapted to Bobby's changing style.

Bobby hurt Feeney once or twice but the kid stayed on his feet and in the game. By the time Bobby was done with the second round the judges had already scored him ahead, by a huge margin.

When Bobby came out of his corner at the start of the third round he fell back into some old habits and it almost seemed as though he had forgotten the wasn't a fight to be Bobby the Brawler but Bobby the Fighter. He didn't keep his hands up and he was using his face to catch punches. It was costing him. Every time he went in close to Feeney, Feeney nailed him right in that unguarded face.

Bobby lost that third round on points but with all the points he had racked up in the first two rounds, the judges gave Bobby the win on points.

Bobby would advance.

He was fighting a little smarter but would it be enough to win the Nationals or carry him in the Pro ranks? No one could be sure that night.

After that fight Bob had a few things to say about his opponent that we found printed in a Lowell Sun article by none other than Dennis Whitton.

"I hurt him a couple of times and he took it. I don't know what kept him up, but he is a tough kid."

When asked about the third round when he was losing the advantage he had the following to say, "I knew I wasn't keeping my hands up. But at that point I knew he wasn't going to hurt me, so I just said if he catches me fine, but I'll get him with two or three good shots while he gets me with one."

There is a special kind of thinking there only a brawler could put forward. He was ok getting hit, and didn't mind, as long as he got to give back shots as well.

He won, and was on his way forward.

THE NATIONALS

Bob advanced to the National Golden Glove Tournament that year. The event was held in Kansas City. Our friend Dennis Whitton of the Lowell Sun wrote a tongue in cheek article about what would happen at that tournament.

"In the 156 pound category Bobby Christakos of Lowell will fight toe to toe for nine minutes, get the decision, collapse from exhaustion, and be carried off in a stretcher, as the crowd boos him wildly."

Thinking about Bob's boxing experience to this point that very much could have happened.

As he was about to leave for the tournament his trainer, Art Ramalho had the following to say, "Bobby's been working really hard in the gym. He's throwing the straight hands now and that will help him here. I think he's going to be just fine."

Bobby was going to fight Jeffrey Wilson in the first round of the National Golden Glove Tournament. Bob really had managed to change his style from brawler to boxer. That was a huge step for him.

When Wilson was introduced the crowd went nuts. He was a very popular local fighter. He was the older brother of a three time local regional champion.

The crowd loved the fight. It was close, it was exciting, and it went back and forth. There were shots that caused the crowd to gasp, wince; no one was sure who was up on points.

The third round ended and they waited. Sweat pouring from the two men, blood from little cuts here and there.

What would they say?

They announced Bob the winner of that round. He had managed to live through one round and fought in a different style. That was huge.

When asked about it Bobby said, "I think the difference was the fact that I really listed to people…I listed to Art Ramalho and my brother Butchy telling me what to do. I was boxing better, I wasn't taking too many wild shots and I was moving good. I never slipped my head as good as I did tonight. Everything just fit into place."

Unfortunately, the next round would result in Bobby running into the man who would eventually win the nationals. But Bobby had learned a valuable lesson in sports, and in life.

Listening to people around you, taking advance and combining it with experience helps in many ways. He may have lost that fight, and not gotten the National Title, but he learned, and that is important.

In this case Bob fought hard and went a long way. He did very well, and, in the end, had learned some valuable lessons that would serve him well in life.

Chapter Twelve

The end of fighting, but not the last fight

Bobby Christakos did not win the national Golden Gloves that year and was reluctant to turn pro just yet. He wanted to keep training as an amateur for at least one more year to work out some of the kinks in his style.

Then, in February 1983 he was back on the card, this time to fight Terry Crowley. This one made him nervous. Terry was not a joke, and he wanted his record to show that he could take on real challengers and win. If he couldn't take on the better amateurs how was he going to handle fighters in the professional ranks?

His nerves were bad despite the fact that he had won a recent fight by decision in a fairly easy bout against Alan Brown in the 156-lb semifinals of the Greater Lowell open tournament.

But, as soon as the bell rang, Bobby was his old self again. He threw haymakers to the body; he landed a punishing uppercut to the head. He was protecting his face well. He knew he could turn pro if he could do this. His shot at a title and the big money was on the line.

He was even listening to Art Ramalho's advice. He was told to stay in close and work the body. Art was even impressed with Bobby's new ability to slip and avoid a beating. That was something that would be absolutely necessary if he were going to turn professional.

He won that fight, the second to last of his amateur career.

Afterwards when asked about his new style he said to a Lowell Sun reporter, "I'm not getting hit no more. I'm working on keeping my hands up. I have to give credit to my brother Butchie for sparring with me and my Father and Dave Ortiz for getting me in shape. I'm getting in better shape but I still need more work. I want to win the title for my father He wants both me and Butchie to win and that would make my father the happiest guy in the world."

February 16, 1983 was to be his final amateur fight in Lowell. His final opponent was to be John Wilkinson of Holyoke.

Right to the very end of Bobby's boxing career the crowds had a love hate relationship with him. Again he was booed as he entered the ring, then cheered for during the fight, only to be booed once again when he won (which he did).

That night Wilkinson won the first round with his brutal left hand, it just pounded away on Bobby from the start. Bobby came back in the second with some cannon-like shots to Wilkinson's face (according to Dennis Whitton). In the third and final round, both of them were exhausted. Bobby being Bobby, got in there and pounded with his exhausted fists and rallied for the win on points.

After the fight Bobby had a lot to say about the booing (which Butchie was also started to get thanks to the family connection), and the crowd in Lowell.

"We [he and Butch] put on the best fights here and they still boo us. We're from Lowell and they know we're going to put on a good fight every night. They should be cheering us and they boo us instead."

"We give 'em everything we have. 110% and they still boo us. And Butchie now. He never did anything wrong to anyone in his life and they boo him. I can't figure it out."

Dennis Whitton conjectured, "Some of the booing is because they are known for hitting so damn hard. If they don't come out and win by KO or unanimous decision they boo all the more."

That was to be the last night Bob fought in Lowell as an amateur. He would only have three fights as a professional before leaving the sport due to an arm injury sustained during an auto accident. But it would not the last Lowell would hear of Bobby Christakos.

WEST END GYM FUNDRAISER

Not long after the Golden Glove Tournament that year, and before the automobile accident, the West End Gym needed to raise money because Art Ramalho didn't charge much to his kids. If they couldn't pay they would never be kicked out, so the gym was always lacking funds. There was to be a fundraiser that year.

The night was going to be a bunch of the fighters from the gym doing exhibition rounds with each other. It was nothing serious, nothing fancy, just a show for the neighborhood and a bunch of guys having fun to raise money for their gym.

There was an early in the evening upset when Golden Gloves Novice Champion Charles Gargone defeated former New England Open Champion Jorge Beltre. The crowd loved it, but the night was not over. The fight everyone was waiting for was the Christakos Brothers.

Brother was about to fight brother.

It was a boxing Civil War.

Bob and Butch were about to get into the ring with each other. What was billed as a fight for fun and charity would turn out to be a family war.

The first thirty seconds they just threw some good natured jabs, and put on a show.

Then, everything changed.

Bob threw a huge left hook to the head.

He claims he did it just to be funny.

Butch was momentarily stunned.

Butch was not laughing.

Then, he recovered and came after his brother with a vengeance.

Butch pounded his brother's ribs like he was Rocky Balboa in the meat packing plant. Bob blocked and came back with an uppercut. This was not for show, this was for family pride. This was for bragging rights at the Thanksgiving table.

When the first round was over they went to their respective corners and listened to no one. They glared at each other across the ring with hatred in their eyes. It was inhuman. They just wanted to get back at each other. It was blood lust. They really wanted to win...both of them. By any means necessary.

This went on to the end of the exhibition as their father just looked on with a smile.

The final bell sounded to end the fight but both Butch and Bobby refused to stop Referee Nike Provetti had to step in and separate the two while the crowd went wild.

It was something those in attendance will never forget.

Brother against brother. Since the Civil War no two brothers have done to each other what those two tried to do.

Then when it was done, they hugged.

They were family again.

The Christakos' always put on a show.

That was to be Bobby's last time in the ring in Lowell, and shortly after would be his final time in the ring ever.

AFTER BOXING

Bob's life after boxing has taken more twists and turns. No life is perfect, there is always tragedy but he has remained a fighter.

Today, Bobby umpires young kids during baseball season, including some for the Lowell Spinners organization.

He is the umpire that takes no garbage. He may hold a record on ejecting parents from little league games for asking for them to "give their kid a break."

There are no freebies in a game when Bobby is the

Ump.

He has had his tragedies in life, he has been arrested, but since meeting his wife has managed to stay out of legal trouble. He has fought in life and is doing just fine.

He survived the loss of his daughter Alexa in 2012 when she was killed in a tragic motorcycle crash.

He now fights the memory of her loss, and the loss of his younger brother Butch who died in his 40s from a heart attack.

Today you can still find Bobby Christakos at the gym, working with a few fighters and working part time for Market Basket to keep himself busy "and out of trouble."

Market Basket is a local grocery store chain and has been the subject of some recent legal fights that make it fit right in there in the city of Lowell. But that is the story for our final chapter.

We will leave the story of Bobby Christakos right here. But the city of Lowell, its residents, and even Market Basket grocery chain fight on. Below Bob can be seen with one of his coworkers at the Market Basket in Lowell Mass.

Chapter Thirteen

Lowell still fights …even for grocery stores

If you have ever spent time in Boston or the surrounding areas you have, without a doubt, seen a DeMoulas or Market Basket grocery store.

There are seventy-seven of them, they are big, and they are everywhere. They are also loved by people looking for a place to grocery shop at a reasonable price without having to be concerned about shopping cards or other membership nonsense.

Market Basket was owned by a family by the name of DeMoulas and was initially called, simply, DeMoulas.

The first DeMoulas grocery store was located in, none other than Lowell, Massachusetts. Yet another first for our fighting little city.

DEMOULAS FAMILY HISTORY

The current head of Market Basket grocery stores is a man by the name of Arthur T. DeMoulas. Arthur's father was a man named Telemachus "Mike" DeMoulas. Mike was a good friend, and frequent visitor to a coffee shop run by none other than Kito Chrostakos, the father of our very own Bobby Christakos.

The DeMoulas family is of Greek-American heritage. It only makes sense that they would spend a great deal of time in the Greek restaurants of the Lowell

Acre. In fact, Arthur T. lived in Lowell until he was a teenager when his family moved to Andover.

How far back do the DeMoulas have roots in Lowell?

There was an Athanasios "Arthur" DeMoulas who was an orphan as a result of the Greco-Turkish War. He moved to the United States, coming through Ellis Island in 1906. From the Island to the Acre. In 1914 he married a woman named Efosene. In 1917 he left a job at a factory he was working in (remember Lowell is a mill town at that point in history) and opened the first DeMoulas Market. DeMoulas would later be renamed as Market Basket.

Remember all of those stories about Bobby's father being a standup guy and doing things like returning the $200 to the woman whose husband had lost the grocery money?

The DeMoulas family, and the residents of Lowell, are the kind of people who would watch out for one another in much the same way.

This wasn't just a Christakos thing, it was more of a Lowell and the Acre thing.

How far back did this take place?

During the Great Depression in 1929, the DeMoulas market gave families who were struggling and on the edge of starvation, free bread with ham and allowed them to purchase groceries on very beneficial credit terms.

Recently, the DeMoulas Market Basket Corporation was the subject of an amazing corporate battle that captured the attention of the entire region. It shows that the fighting spirit is still in those residents of

Lowell.

To the Market Basket customers and employee this was a fight of right vs. wrong. It is the kind of thing that New Englanders, in fact all Americans, get all worked up for.

At issue was the removal of Arthur T. DeMoulas as the company's CEO by his cousin Arthur S. DeMoulas. For sure, keeping the Arthurs straight can get confusing, but bear with us. Arthur T. made some bold moves as the CEO such as giving their customers a 4% cash back bonus on their groceries and had given employees stock in the company.

Shortly after the decision of Arthur T's removal was announced, employees walked out. Not only was this a company thing but the customers were so loyal to Artie T. that they refused to shop at Market Basket, even though most of the stores remained open through the six weeks of turmoil for the company.

It may seem cliché at this point, but the fight over control of the Market Basket chain was much the same as Bobby's fight for respect as a Boxer and Lowell's fight to thrive as a major American city. But that comparison is so appropriate this fight should be included for the record.

THE FIRING OF ARTIE T.

There had been decades of resentment and the occasional legal dispute between the two cousins who controlled the Market Basket Corporation. There was one Arthur S. and, of course, Arthur T. DeMoulas. The lawsuits were seen as really petty spats originating from Arthur S. who thought he should have more shares in the company.

These legal arguments came to a head in 2013 when Arthur S. gained support of another majority shareholder and decided to take the company in a different direction.

The conflict wasn't over a difference of opinion over the better direction of the company in the long run; it was about how a few people at the top tried to cash out quickly while one man wanted to preserve the discounted prices for his customers and benefits for his employees.

One of the ways Market Basket had managed to keep prices down and benefits up, even in hard economic times, was by managing overhead. One of the main ways they accomplished low overhead was to own the shopping centers and real estate of their locations rather than rent space. In the end this was cheaper but required a very large cash investment.

Arthur S. had this idea that the company should sell off the current real estate holdings and then lease back the space from the new owners. This would allow the current majority shareholders to go home with an enormous amount of cash immediately. IT would also result in an increase in prices for their customers and fewer benefits for their employees.

Arthur T. said he would not stand for this and he was removed as CEO.

Now there was real trouble.

The employees and more surprisingly, the customers stepped up to the plate and rebelled. This wasn't planned by some mysterious group, it was spontaneous.

THE FIGHT AND A VICTORY

After six weeks of reporting breaking news on the Artie T. saga in 2014, Valley Patriot publisher Tom Duggan wrote a column encapsulating the Market Basket drama from the perspective of the customers and employees.

CARTOON © Dave Sullivan, Dracut MA, & The Valley Patriot 9/14

"Artie T. is an Inspiration to Us All."

By, Tom Duggan, from the Valley Patriot Newspaper with permission

It was like a drama from a Hollywood movie. The "good" Arthur T. DeMoulas vs. the "evil" Arthur S. DeMoulas is how the scenario played in the news and on social media.

The evil cousin, consumed with greed, profit, and the bottom line tries to take over a supermarket chain, while the good cousin was fighting for lower prices for his customers and better benefits for his employees.

When the "good" cousin Artie "T" was fired by the board, workers began to protest but more importantly the customers of DeMoulas-Market Baskets began to boycott the store. Days dragged into weeks as empty stores with empty shelves made everyone question the future of our favorite "More for Your Dollar", family supermarket.

Why did the workers and the customers take such a bold stand for Artie "T" and boycott his dismissal?

Talking to the protesters every day it became clear on day one that Arthur T. DeMoulas put his workers and his customers first.

Employees happily recounted how Artie "T" had helped them during the death of a family member, showing up at their homes with baby formula after the birth of a baby, and donating money and/or food to workers who were going through tough times. The stories were so numerous it would take all forty pages of this newspaper to recount even half of them.

As a small business owner myself, I was in awe at the way Artie "T" treated his employees but I was even more in awe that, in the selfish narcissistic culture we live in today, that the employees and customers actually recognized and appreciated what Artie "T" had done for all of them and what he truly represented to the entire community.

It takes a special person to evoke that kind of selfless loyalty among an American population more consumed with Brittany Spears, weekend partying, their cell phones, and MTV reality shows.

But somehow Artie "T" pulled it off. He not only had the full support of his employees and his customers, but also was able to make a huge personal sacrifice to purchase the entire Market Basket Supermarket chain from the "evil" Artie "S" and within 24 hours of his announcement, the workers and the customers were back.

We can all learn a lesson from this saga over Market Basket.

Despite what the media promotes every day on TV and in movies, being a cold, greedy businessman who only cares about profit and bottom line does not make one successful. Having the respect and love of the people you employ and the customers you service does.

We wish there were more Artie T's out there running major corporations and small businesses. As someone who covered this story from beginning to end, I can tell you that the new saying here at The Valley Patriot Corporate Office is "How would Artie "T" handle this" any time a tough situation arises.

Artie "T" not only inspired his customers and his employees but he is now an inspiration to all of us to "put people first" and bottom line second.

That's why at next year's Valley Patriot Annual BASH! (March 20, 2015), we plan on giving out our very first ever "Artie T. DeMoulas Scholarship" to an employee or former employee of Market Basket, among the other scholarships and awards we give away at our yearly celebration.

We also encourage other businesses to do the same, so that future generations will never forget how Artie T. saved his employees jobs, the supermarket chain, and made personal sacrifices every single day to make that happen.

While we hardly expect a man as busy as Artie "T" to be reading our little monthly newspaper, it is our hope that the employees and the customers of Market Basket will pass the word along that we at The Valley Patriot recognize his efforts and appreciate all he has done. We are going to do everything possible to follow in his footsteps to contribute to the community the way he has for so many years.

Thank you Artie "T" and thank you to the workers, customers and food vendors for showing the rest of the country what caring for others is really all about.

Thank you as well to all the people behind the scenes who helped the cause of having Artie "T" restored as CEO, including but not limited to, State Senator Barry Finegold, State Rep. Diana DiZoglio, Lawrence Mayor Dan Rivera, Lowell Mayor Rodney Elliott, State Senator Katy Ives, State Rep. Marcos Devers, Congresswoman Niki Tsongas, and the dozens of local city councilors, selectmen and state officials who saw a good man being treated badly and stood up for what was right.

You are all an inspiration to humanity. The efforts and accomplishments you undertook to make this happen will not be forgotten for a long time.

Now let's take this lesson of Arthur T. DeMoulas and pay it forward!

Let's make Artie "T" proud!

Photo: Tom Duggan, © Valley Patriot 2014

The protests were the fighting spirit of Lowell come to life. It was not only effective but it was peaceful, within the law, spontaneous and amazing to see firsthand.

****

WHAT IS NEXT FOR BOBBY, AND LOWELL

Well, that is a tough question to answer.

No one can say for sure what the future holds. But some things are certain. The citizens of Lowell will continue to embody that fighting spirit that served Bobby in the ring, and helped build the city of Lowell.

The people of the Acre in Lowell will continue to fight to make their neighborhood a better to live.

Artite T. will continue to fight for his employees and his customers as he always has, with that unique fighting spirit that; saved the Market Basket chain, earned Bobby Christakos five Golden Gloves, and has brought the city of Lowell back from the brink of chaos many times over the years.

This book is dedicated to the citizens of Lowell and the employees of Market Basket for banding together and saving the supermarket chain as well as Arthur T. DeMoulas.

VALLEY PATRIOT PEOPLE OF THE YEAR! MARKET BASKET EMPLOYEES! (12/14)

"If anyone deserves to be named Person (or People) of the Year it's the dedicated employees of Market Basket! From the guys who stock the shelves to the gal at the meat counter, to the truck drivers and cashiers, the employees of Market Basket stood up for Artie "T" and forced what many thought impossible - the departure of Artie "S" and the full control of Market Basket in the hands of Artie "T". As loyal Market Basket shoppers, the Valley Patriot wants to thank Artie "T" but even more importantly the army of loyal employees who helped save Market Basket as our More for your Dollar supermarket! Pictured above with State Rep Diana DiZoglio (2nd from left) are: (L-R) Manny Ma of Lowell, Angel Porter of North Andover, Ken Mercer of Tewksbury and Carolina Agudealo of South Lawrence all from the North Andover Market Basket store.

About the Authors:

Tom Duggan, Jr. is President and publisher of The Valley Patriot Newspaper in North Andover Massachusetts, covering 51 cities and towns in MA and NH. He also owns valleypatriot.com a daily news website.

A former member of the Lawrence School Committee, and the former political director for Mass. Citizens Alliance, Tom also has lectures about politics, media bias and corruption in the news media.

He is a 1990 Police Survivor and hosts the Paying Attention! Radio Program on 980WCAP in Lowell, Massachusetts.

Timothy Imholt was an enlisted soldier in the Army was honorably discharged in 1996. After receiving his discharge at the age of 24, attended the University of North Texas where he earned a B.S. and Ph.D. in Physics, all on his own dime.

Today Tim is a family man, married to his lovely wife Jean. Together they are raising their three children, two small boys and baby girl. Tim also have an older daughter from a previous marriage who is currently attending college in Texas.

He has authored several books including the best seller "Forest of Assassins" available on Amazon.com.

Made in the USA
Lexington, KY
05 February 2015